W9-AJQ-331

Lee Smith

Twayne's United States Authors Series

Frank Day, Editor
Clemson University

TUSAS 592

Lee Smith
Photograph copyright 1988 by Jerry Bauer

Lee Smith

Dorothy Combs Hill

Georgetown University

Twayne Publishers • New York

Maxwell Macmillan Canada • Toronto

Maxwell Macmillan International • New York Oxford Singapore Sydney

*To my mother, Lucille Walters Combs, and my
father, Kenneth Bickley Combs,
for giving me life*

*And to Doctor Herbert Proctor and Doctor
Michelle Thiet for giving it back to
me when it was almost taken*

Lee Smith

Dorothy Combs Hill

Copyright 1992 by Twayne Publishers

Twayne Publishers
Macmillan Publishing Company
866 Third Avenue
New York, New York 10022

Maxwell Macmillan Canada, Inc.
1200 Eglinton Avenue East
Suite 200
Don Mills, Ontario M3C 3N1

Macmillan Publishing Company is part of the Maxwell Communication Group of Companies.

Library of Congress Cataloging-in-Publication Data

Hill, Dorothy Combs
 Lee Smith / Dorothy Combs Hill.
  p. cm. – (Twayne's United States authors series; TUSAS 592)
 Includes bibliographical references and index.
 ISBN 0-8057-7640-0 (alk. paper)
 1. Smith, Lee, 1944- – Criticism and interpretation. 2. Women in literature. I. Title. II. Series: Twayne's United States authors series; TUSAS 592.
PS3569.M5376Z68 1991
813.54 – dc20   91-36800
                                                         CIP

10 9 8 7 6 5 4 3 2 1

Printed in the United States of America.

Contents

Preface

On the writing of Lee Smith, a colleague at the University of North Carolina at Chapel Hill once remarked to me that "any work that has a cheerleader as an artist figure is doomed." It struck me then how blinded we all are, even the best of us, by cultural constructs that trivialize the roles traditionally assigned to women, even while we all starve for what these roles provide.

Under a humorous – often heavily erotic or deceptively banal – surface, the serious issues of female isolation and identity constitute the core of Smith's work. Behind and underneath all of Lee Smith's writing is the worth of the world of women, as well as this world's almost unbearable loneliness. The controlling myths of our culture dismiss or revile women. There is almost no way a woman can grow and develop, except as a mother, without becoming a male because the standards of maturation are male. The deity, too, is culturally imaged as male. Saint Augustine, whose ideas are so deeply embedded in our culture, thought that women had to change themselves into men at the moment of death to gain admittance to heaven. By the very roles we assign women, we still belittle and degrade them. And there tends not to be much comfort. As Dorothy Dinnerstein points out in her brilliant 1977 study, *The Mermaid and the Minotaur: Sexual Arrangements and Human Malaise*, adult males can return to the original comforting body, the female body, for solace, whereas women cannot.

I first began to understand what Smith was doing in her fiction, really, when I overheard her telling someone about a dream she had had the night before. She was on a cruise ship, bound for Greece. While the others were exhilarated by wind and sea on deck, she had to go below and do the wash. The washing machine, she said, was tiny and would hold only one or two garments at a time. So even though the garments were small, feminine things, like bras and slips, the task was endless. She never got to leave the ship. The others went ashore and toured Greece without her. When they returned, she asked them, these lucky ones, "What were the statues like?"

Then I understood. Left out of the myths, assigned to small and menial tasks, terribly alone, and still called whores of Babylon anyway, women were doomed. Smith, in her fiction, tries to save them.

Acknowledgments

I would like to thank the following persons: my access to myself and everything else, Elaine; my hope, Jonathan; my heart's darling, never turning away, Jack Murrah; my beloved, Holly Larsen; my horseman, Clarence Tyrone Coakley; my lion, Bryan Matthew Hill; my enduring friend, Judson J. Van Wyk; my constant comfort, Carol Fleischer Kent; my thread in the ocean, Patricia O'Connor; my daily bread, Doris Eley; my history, Dixie Bowden; my coffee girl, Annie Deans; my grocery girl, Porthia Douglas; my main mailman, George Warren; my resident elf, George Hazelton; and my shimmering crystal, who will make it, Christal Edwards. Finally, my inexpressible gratitude goes to Barbara Sutton, the editor at Twayne Publishers who helped me reconstruct this manuscript after the destruction of the original in the crash of a U.S. Mail plane in Hartford, Connecticut, on 2 May 1991.

Finally, I acknowledge my own Red One, Ruth Cates Baird. Three times my teacher, she taught me in eleventh grade at Oak Ridge High how to write, in twelfth grade how to read. Slim and elegant, she was demanding and relentless. But she was something more. For the sustaining vision – with impact – came earlier, at Pine Valley Elementary, where she was my third-grade teacher. Vibrant and dynamic, with her shock of red hair, she sat on the edge of her desk swinging her long leg tipped by a mule slipper. ("Mule" is from the Latin *mulleus*, red or purple shoe.) One day I ran off the playground early and burst into the classroom. She sat at her desk against the window, holding an open compact, splashing red lipstick onto her sensuous mouth, and I was set free.

The following are quoted in the text by permission: "Debris of Life and Mind," copyright 1947 by Wallace Stevens. Reprinted from *The Collected Poems of Wallace Stevens* by permission of Alfred A. Knopf, Inc. Excerpts from *The Meaning of Aphrodite*, copyright 1978 by Paul Friedrich. Reprinted by permission of the University of Chicago.

Chronology

1944   Lee Marshall Smith born 1 November in Grundy, Buchanan County, Virginia, the only child of Ernest Lee Smith, whose family goes back four generations in Grundy, and Virginia Elizabeth Marshall Smith, from the island of Chincoteague on Virginia's eastern shore.

1944-1960   Spends girlhood in Grundy.

1961-1963   Attends St. Catherine's School in Richmond, Virginia.

1963-1967   Attends Hollins College; spends junior year in France; has internship at the *Richmond News Leader* with chief editorial writer James J. Kilpatrick.

1967   Wins $3,000 award for first novel, *The Last Day the Dogbushes Bloomed*. Marries poet James Seay on 17 June.

1968   *The Last Day the Dogbushes Bloomed* published.

1968-1969   Reporter for *Tuscaloosa News*, Tuscaloosa, Alabama.

1969   *The Last Day the Dogbushes Bloomed* published in paperback.

1969-1970   Feature writer, film critic, and editor of *Tuscaloosa News* Sunday magazine.

1971   *Something in the Wind* published.

1971-1974   English teacher, Harpeth Hall School, Nashville, Tennessee.

1973   *Fancy Strut* published.

1975-1977   English teacher, Carolina Friends School, in Virginia.

1976   Writer-in-residence, Hollins College, spring semester.

1977   Receives Distinguished Alumna Award, St. Catherine's
                School. Instructor in creative writing, Continuing Ed-
                ucation, Duke University, Durham, North Carolina.

1978-1981   Lecturer in fiction writing, University of North Carolina
                at Chapel Hill.

1979   Wins O. Henry Award for "Mrs. Darcy Meets the Blue-
                Eyed Stranger at the Beach" (*Carolina Quarterly*,
                Spring-Summer 1978).

1979-1980   Director of a summer writing workshop for the Univer-
                sity of Virginia in Abingdon.

1980   *Black Mountain Breakdown* published.

1981   *Cakewalk* published. Wins O. Henry Award for
                "Between the Lines" (*Carolina Quarterly*, Winter
                1980). Instructor in fiction writing, Cumberland Valley
                Writers Conference Summer Workshop, Nashville.

1981-1985   Assistant professor of English, North Carolina State
                University, Raleigh.

1982   Divorced from James Seay. *Black Mountain Break-
                down* and *Cakewalk* published in paperback.

1983   *Oral History* published, wins Sir Walter Raleigh Award
                for Fiction.

1984   Receives North Carolina Award for Fiction.

1985   Associate professor of English, North Carolina State
                University. Marries syndicated columnist Harold B.
                Crowther, Jr., on 29 June. *Family Linen* published.
                Lee Smith Festival, Emory and Henry College, 10-11
                October.

1986   Is one of seven southern writers responding to the
                question "Does southern literature still exist?" in Au-
                gust *Harper's*. *Black Mountain Breakdown, Cake-
                walk, Oral History*, and *Family Linen* issued together
                in paperback. First Lime Kiln Arts production of the
                play *Ear Rings*, an adaptation of *Oral History* by Don
                Baker (songs by Tommy Thompson, with Jack Her-
                rick).

1987   Wins John Dos Passos Award for Literature. *Fancy Strut* published in paperback.

1988   *Fair and Tender Ladies* and *Bob, a Dog* (limited edition) published. Virginia Marshall Smith dies in April.

1989   Delivers Susan B. Anthony Speech, "Helping Mama Make It through the Night: Women in Art," at North Carolina State University, 20 February. Gives benefit reading for PEN International at the Folger Shakespeare Library, Washington, D.C., 24 February. Delivers Baylies-Willey Lecture for National Women's History Month, "But Is It Art? A Lecture on Woman and Creativity," at Hollins College, 29 March. For *Fair and Tender Ladies* wins W. D. Weatherford Award for Appalachian Literature (Berea College, Berea, Kentucky) and Appalachian Writers Award (both in April). Member of Advisory Board, North Carolina Writers Network. Visiting professor of English, Virginia Commonwealth University, Richmond, fall semester. *Fair and Tender Ladies* published in paperback.

1989-1990   Barbara Smith and Mark Hunter write and produce *Ivy Rowe*, a play based on *Fair and Tender Ladies*; it opens in Tampa in 1989, and Smith and Hunter take it to New York in 1990.

1990   *Me and My Baby View the Eclipse* published. Steering Committee, Center for Documentary Studies, Duke University. Receives Lyndhurst Fellowship.

1991   First recipient, Robert Penn Warren Prize. Tenth Annual Southern Writers' Symposium, 27-28 September: "Lee Smith: Storyteller," Methodist College, Fayetteville, North Carolina, for which Lee Yopp produces a play based on *Family Linen*. Receives PEN/Faulkner Award for "Mom," a short story collected in *Me and My Baby View the Eclipse*. Gives PEN/Faulkner reading for prize winners, 12 December, Library of Congress, Washington, D.C.

Introduction

Literature springs from a wound. Critical acclaim attests to the style and flair, the competence, the passion, and the urgency with which the wound is dressed. Popular acclaim is recognition of our mutual wounding, and it acknowledges the efficacy of the treatment, at least for temporary relief. It is always a secret wound, something we are defended even against seeing, for otherwise it would not be necessary to apply the salve secretly, under the guise of fiction. To rid ourselves of the pain, of this wound we admit neither having nor feeling, we inflict the selfsame wound on others. We pretend that it is necessary wounding. We pretend that it is necessary for participation in culture. We pretend that it is necessary for normalcy even. The reason it is so horrible to look at directly is that we, along with those we love and who love us, have inflicted the wound on ourselves.

The wound that the whole important body of Lee Smith's work redresses is the terrible cultural wound inflicted on creative women that keeps them from understanding themselves and even denies them any access to themselves. They have no access to themselves, neither in their own unfree imaginations nor in collective institutions. There is no form in which they can recognize themselves, no form in which others can recognize them, certainly not without unsexing or deforming them. The socializing process teaches them that they can find themselves in connection to others. But it is not so, and the yearning continues, and the pain continues. And what they are yearning for, what they are forever blocked from, is themselves. The ache never goes away.

Lee Smith's life is so phenomenal, her message so radical, that it hardly seems permissible to speak of the things she speaks of, because they go straight to the core of our cultural constructions of the sexual and the sacred, our two most closely defended – and, sadly, artificially separated – domains. She gets away with it because her surface dazzles – funny, fetching, come-hither. Both her popular and critical successes have been enormous. Once she draws us in, she remains such a chatty, apparently harmless, even banal guide, pointing to this or that distraction while talking away madly, that we do not feel the hand groping to probe the wound. If we did, we would not allow the healing touch. The wound is so deep and ancient that we have come to think it necessary for existence and have built all our institutions around it. We even think it gives us life, for we think it makes motherhood possible. Certainly it guaranteed a permanent serving class.

I sensed but could not uncover the wound until I read Paul Friedrich's *The Meaning of Aphrodite*.[1] Two nights later–if we let the mind go it will find its way–I awoke at two o'clock in the morning, and it all became clear. I knew the identity of Red Emmy, rising naked from the pool of water, her hair a red rain. I knew the identity of Dory, a girl so lovely as to take your breath away, while all the leaves of autumn swirled about her, red and orange and gold. And I knew why Crystal shattered. I knew because, even before Friedrich gave me names for them, even before Lee Smith gave me images of them, I had already seen them in my lifetime. In the pages that follow I reveal these identities and explore the territory with the light given to me by Friedrich–cultural anthropologist, linguist, poet, and specialist in Homeric Greek. Nor do I imply that Smith was guided by any such light. I am quite sure that she did not consciously employ the archetypes. Rather, they arose from a full mind and an imagination that fought to free itself from cultural constraints, fought to imagine the female as full and whole–sexual, sacred, active. Haltingly, she found her way across the rough terrain of received mythologies and cramped orthodoxies. Always interested in mythic roles for women, Smith had to reinvent them. Asked by Virginia A. Smith if she was aware of what she is doing in her fiction, Lee Smith answered with an anecdote she had just heard Clyde Egerton use to answer the same question: "It's like when you are a duck and you are flying in a 'V,' you don't know you're in the 'V.' Somebody else has to be down on the ground to see that."[2]

Smith found the raw materials, hidden like gems, in the Celtic song and story of her native Appalachian mountains. Celtic myth, predating Greek myth, goes back to an earlier stratum with stronger, more active images of women. Before the Indo-European sky god came Inanna, the Sumerian Queen of Heaven. Zeus supplants her. In Greek mythology, Aphrodite–whose main function, like Inanna's, is sex–is told by Zeus not to interfere with war, so those domains are separated. In Roman mythology, Venus is told to restrict herself to marriage. The domain kept shrinking. Of course, in Christian iconography the only sacred female is the virgin mother, not only a completely passive model but a biologically impossible one. My argument is not that Smith deliberately reinvented the powerful goddess figures eclipsed by patriarchy. (As she has explained to Virginia Smith, that would be manufacturing, not writing.) My argument is, rather, that the myths themselves stood for psychological complexes that Smith, through her imagination and out of necessity, reinvented.

It took a huge act of imagination, a lifetime of writing, for Smith to find healing images. The inflicting of the wound has been slow, long, and deep. The sacred sexual female was found so potent, so alarming, and so alluring that not only did we stop worshiping her, we denied her existence. Thus did our joy–the joy of us all, male and female–end and punishment begin. The search for the identity of the sacred sexual female is taking place in our culture now. But the only collective form in which we find a durable representation of this identity, the sacred sexual female, is in literature. In the long search a lifetime of writing is, Lee Smith finds her and shows her to us all, with the healing power of language.

Smith says that she writes for self-repair. The serious issues of female isolation and identity make up the core of her work. Her "central characters are primarily women, and her fiction is impressive as a record of the psychological dislocations that have occurred in women during periods of rapid change."[3] She elucidates the female psyche in landscapes and homes jarred by increasing complexity and change attended by bewilderment and pain, and her fiction is a struggle to find healing and reconciliation. Critical and popular response testify to the reparative possibilities of her fiction for us all. "Many writers are considering America's pain," concludes a *Library Journal* article on North Carolina writers, including Smith.[4] These writers "are presently grabbing our attention because they so effectively illuminate our current quandaries . . . [and] are writing stories that help us understand ourselves" (Hoffert, 48).

Smith's writing evokes a variety of comparisons and reactions, alongside the predictable invocation of the names of Faulkner, Welty, O'Connor, and McCullers. Thulani Davis, characterizing Smith as the best of contemporary southern women writers, mused, "Lee Smith

has been compared to Faulkner and McCullers, but she writes with
such joy and laughing sensuality about Virginia/Kentucky hill people
that she could also be said to have an Appalachian streak of [García]
Márquez."[5]

Newsweek reached outside literature to assess Smith's impact:
"Lee Smith's novels are as consciously 'women's fiction' as anything
you might run across in *Redbook* or *McCall's*, but she opens the
genre up and makes it seem expansive. Her work has a mixture of
lyricism and sexual boldness that makes you go outside of writing, to
the work of actresses and women singers, for comparison."[6] One
thinks of such women who assert the truth and value of female experience as actresses Meryl Streep, Glenn Close, and Sonia Braga (the
latter of Smith's favorite movie, *The Kiss of the Spider Woman*) and,
yes, even Madonna, in her "Like a Prayer," "Express Yourself," and
"Cherish" videos.

This book is a study of the female imagination and how it is operating in our time as seen in the fiction of Lee Smith. In his innova-
tive work *Orientalism*, Edward Said has emphasized and analyzed
the ways in which the literary imagination is shaped by and hence
colludes with constructions of power. My work goes along with and
yet lies outside these emphases. I address the ways in which people
on the margins of power structures and cultures can burst out of cultural constructs to create new images.

This breaking out, this bursting forth, has been analyzed in the
work of some Third World writers, but here I address it within the
Western context itself, tracing it through a southern woman writer
who is liminal[7] in various and related ways. For uncovering this dy-
namism I have used the theories of anthropologist Victor Turner,
whose analysis on the role of liminality in the construction of rituals
is equally applicable to the construction of literature in changing
times. If we apply his theories to writers who come from "borders"
we can see how they transgress, overcome, and sometimes transcend
abiding structures and learn something about identity and culture in
observing how they frame new constructs. Imaginative work from the
"borderlands" of gender, class, race, and geography often questions
existing cultural constructs and seeks new syntheses.

It is obvious by now that for my analysis I draw from various but
not unrelated fields. Introducing his study of Aphrodite, Friedrich
states, "I have tried to cross boundaries, to poach in well-stocked

scholarly preserves, to break up standard categories of analysis, and to explore and integrate the insights of many diverse but indispensable fields, such as psychology and Indo-European linguistics. This reflects my own background, a horror at parochialism, academic vested interests, and prejudice of any sort, and a personal belief in a pursuit that transcends particularities in the search for knowledge and the heart's meaning" (Friedrich, 8).

I too have drawn on diversity for my study of Smith's fiction, including a background in language and linguistics, training as a medievalist, immersion in current controversies in literary criticism, a sisterhood with cultural anthropology, an affinity for theology, and my own provenance in Smith's Appalachian coal-mining region along the Kentucky-Virginia border. I have needed all these tools and more to keep up with Smith's fiction in its long search through particularities to find a language of the heart that not only tells the heart's meaning but also illuminates the heart's link to the mind's grandeur.[8]

Chapter One

The Search for a Language

Tongues of Fire

Lee Smith describes her novella "Tongues of Fire" (1990) as "probably as close to autobiography as I will ever write."[1] The story is of a girl whose feelings are strangled by a mother rigidly dedicated to keeping up appearances, especially after the girl's father suffers a nervous breakdown. To find the intensity her spirit craves, the daughter turns to books. Only in the experience of reading can her spirit feel wild and free.

It is this desire – to find a release for the intensity of her spirit – and this form of release – reading – that Smith admits as autobiographical.[2] She says that she was impelled to write not by the storytelling tradition so often used to explain the genesis of southern writers but by her hunger for reading. "I always had my nose in a book," she says, "and I would read anything – the *Black Stallion* books, *Johnny Tremaine*, *Little Women*, the *Reader's Digest Condensed Books*, the Bible – I loved to go to church" (pers. comm., 1989).

The hunger is configured as spiritual as well as emotional, both in Smith's recollection and in "Tongues of Fire." The protagonist of that story, who lists a similar catalog of books turned to for emotional release, becomes fascinated by the ecstatic utterances of the mother of a rural schoolmate. The mother, who belongs to a rural sect that speaks in tongues, explains that "Tongues of fire just come down on my head."[3]

"I envy this," Smith told an amused audience in an address at Virginia Commonwealth University, "and aspire to it more than I can tell you" (Richmond, 1989). No theosophy is required to see why the idea of ecstatic release of language would appeal to a born writer. Smith grew up in, but not exactly of, a culture where she witnessed

1

such phenomena. Her admiration for and distance from her characters is part of what makes her work possible. "If you feel at home in a culture," she says, "you don't write" (pers. comm., 1989). She went on to tell the Virginia audience that she too had become fascinated with speaking in tongues when she was about 13. When she gave it a try in public, her parents packed her off to camp in West Virginia. There she "outfoxed everyone by having a fit at an Episcopal vespers service." She was immediately declared "disturbed" and "homesick" and was sent to the camp's infirmary, where her parents phoned and promised her a Pekingese if she would only "shape up and stay for the rest of the term" (Richmond, 1989).

Smith's anecdote is typical of her humor and of her imaginative impulse. The gap between inchoate spiritual longing and proffered material substitutes, in her fiction as in life, is both hilarious and tragic. This gap becomes particularly poignant when it involves parents' attempts to offer their children a substitute for a need they know they cannot fill or that reminds them too painfully of what they long ago gave up. When Crystal, the troubled and troubling protagonist of *Black Mountain Breakdown* (1980), suffers a profound spiritual crisis after the death of her father, her compulsive and materialistically oriented mother wishes she would just eat some Jell-O. Smith's fullest characters, like Ivy Rowe of *Fair and Tender Ladies* (1988), combine spiritual intensity and the capacity for imaginative flight with down-to-earth common sense and the "guts and grace" to endure (pers. comm., 1989).

The girl who read for an intensity missing in the world around her but craved by her spirit became the woman who experiences her feelings "most deeply when I am writing."[4] The search for a language of the heart denied by polite society is conducted by both Smith's fictive characters and her fictive language. Finding such a language is tantamount to finding the self; mouthing the words of others is tantamount to losing the self. In addition, Smith's fiction continually explores image versus reality. These two impulses converge in her fiction, which turns on the way in which language articulates with reality, either to open it up or to screen it or to open oneself up to it or screen oneself from it. Whichever way this dialectic is framed, in Smith's fiction language is nodal.

The situation into which Smith puts her protagonist in "Tongues of Fire" is not, and need not be read as, autobiographical. It is, in fact, instantly recognizable as one version of a fundamental conflict: the cold claims of society versus the claims of the human heart. This is where literature can do its healing work. Some of Smith's characters succeed or fail depending on whether they avail themselves of the healing power of language. The thread runs true from the nine-year-old Susan who turns to spelling in times of crisis; to Brooke, lost in the mystery of herself and working crossword puzzles, searching for a clue; to all those characters who first betray and then lose their essential selves by succumbing to rotten diction, reaching for clichés, and saying what is expected of them; to social pretense characterized by such speech acts as dropping the Anglo-Saxon *live* for the French *reside*. The thread does not stop here; it also runs from the incantatory magic of *Oral History* (1983) with its "wild song"[5] to *Fair and Tender Ladies*, "as true to life as the high, sweet sound of mountain music in a gathering dusk."[6]

Smith, whose writing is as often composed in her head as it is on paper, has little patience with writing rituals. While cooking, chauffeuring children, or driving to work she does what she calls "prewriting," thinking it out in her head. Finding plotting most difficult – and this is what critics have faulted her on – she thinks up characters and then puts them in situations to see how they will react. She then does a lengthy outline, sometimes a hundred pages or more, before she sits down to write. Once she is ready to begin, she writes the last sentence first, tapes it up on the kitchen wall, and then writes toward that ending. The last sentence of *Fair and Tender Ladies* – "oh I was young then, and I walked in my body like a Queen"[7] – was on her kitchen wall for three years (pers. comm., 1989).

She does little or no revision. There is a certain kind of polish, she says, that she does not want to put on her work.[8] It is ordinary language – the colloquial, the language "of communion and community" – with which she works. In that sense she answers to Stanley Cavell's "democratization of the whole philosophic enterprise."[9] Her uncanny ability to reproduce common language sometimes confuses readers, such as Christopher Lehmann-Haupt: "For just a fleeting instant I found myself wondering if the ineptitude of Jennifer's prose was intentional on the author's part. I really ought to be ashamed of myself. . . . I should be ashamed because what Lee Smith does best of all in . . . [*Oral History*] is to capture the voices that tell her story."[10] Others, such as Thulani Davis, more quickly catch the connections under an often banal surface: "The more stylish writers deliver something startling and sharp, but Smith deceives with simplicity. Everything seems so straightforward, even superficial at times, and yet she moves you. She connects" (Davis, 11). Still others, like fellow southern writer Doris Betts, perceive something lurking beneath Smith's humorous, erotic surface and surmise, "It's a dark vision she has."[11]

Smith believes it a mistake to think of an audience when she writes. In fact, she believes it a mistake for any fiction writer, lest self-betrayal sneak in on one side or manipulation on the other. In addition to her stricture that the writer write only for herself for the work to be true, Smith cautions that a writer is not necessarily someone who is publishing. Rather, a writer is someone who is writing. Her closets, she says, are filled with writing that will never be published. If there is a message she delivers in her frequent talks to young and would-be writers, in lectures and readings and workshops, it is to be true to one's own imagination. She writes for herself, to contact and express the passion and intensity she found expressed in the word when she was a child. Then the peculiar alchemy of art takes place, in which the most deeply felt personal obsession becomes the most universal. The resultant miracle is that a book springing from memoirs of one's own Appalachian ancestors winds up on display in a Paris bookstore. But inner connection comes first. Reviewing Ellen Gilchrist's *Drunk with Love,* Smith paraphrased the words of a Gilchrist character like a mantra: "Myself, I admire passion. I have always admired passion."[12]

Lee Smith Country

Lee Marshall Smith was born just after midnight 31 October-1 November 1944 to Ernest Lee Smith and Virginia Elizabeth Marshall Smith in Grundy, Virginia, a Buchanan County town (population 1,699) deep in the mountains of Appalachian coal country near the Kentucky state line. The 36-year-old father and 37-year-old mother had been told that they could never have a child. Their baby girl was a complete surprise. Smith's Aunt Millie said she just missed being born on Halloween by a hair (pers. comm., 1991). It is fascinating to speculate on the character-shading effects of having one's birthday on the cusp of All Hallow Even – a wild pagan holiday in which spirits are seen dancing in the flesh and even witches are celebrated – and All Souls' Day. This is the very territory – the interstitial place – all Smith's fiction will explore. (Her forthcoming novel, for which Smith did research on country music families, is to be titled *Devil's Dream*, which is the title of a fiddle tune.) The border crossed between 31 October and 1 November – a spatiotemporal boundary marking the mystery of our separation of flesh and spirit, of sexual and sacred – is the territory of Smith's fiction.

Ernest Smith was born in Grundy on 17 September 1909 into a family that went back in the rugged frontier territory as far as anyone could remember, at least four generations. The family memory recounted the days when the mountains were wild – when panther, deer, and bear roamed – recollected the heydays of the lumber trade when the great forests were felled, and told of the digging of the mines, with boom followed by bust. Smith's father was county treasurer for 40 years. His grandfather, a trader, was murdered, shot while on horseback. After fighting in World War II, Smith invested himself in ownership and management of a Ben Franklin five-and-dime in Grundy. By the time his daughter was growing up, he was among the town's leading citizens. Lee spent her childhood surrounded by the Smith clan, including numerous cousins who were her playmates and companions. She was heir to a rich supply of stories and had ample opportunity for her imagination to develop. "Only children have a lot of time alone," she says, "and all I ever did was read and write."[13]

Virginia Marshall Smith was born one of six children in 1908 on Chincoteague, an island off the coast of Virginia famous for its wild ponies. Her family had branched out from Baltimore and settled along the eastern shores of Maryland and Virginia to Richmond. Her father, who was in the oyster trade, committed suicide before her fifth birthday. She was not told what happened, only that he was "sick." Gig (pronounced "jig"), as her family called her, grew up with her mother, Annie Turlington Marshall, and her brothers and sisters, in Chincoteague. (The old family name, Turlington, shows up not only in the name of Smith's second son, but in her fiction as well; portions of journals passed down for generations in that family appear in her work.) Graduating from James Madison College, Gig met

Ernest Smith when her sister Marion married his uncle. After an intense courtship they eloped and came home to Grundy. For many
years she taught home economics at the Grundy high school. She
brought with her an idea of class and gentility, a notion of how life
should be lived gleaned from Richmond and Baltimore, and a snob-
bishness toward her husband's native region that never quite left
her, even though she remained in Grundy until her death. Despite
her aspirations to gentility, Smith's mother was from a marginal location too. The island of Chincoteague, like the Appalachians, is linked
to wild nature. Furthermore, islands, like mountains, were sacred to
Aphrodite and were often sites for her temples. Islands and mountains are sacred boundary zones between land and water, land and
sky. Both Smith's parents, then, were from fringes.

Lee Smith grew up with two traditions in deep conflict, bridged
by the equally deep love her parents bore for each other. They found
something in common. Her father was "kind of a maverick. He had
gone away to William and Mary to play football one season and ac-
quired some notions," and he married her mother, who was "what
they refer to in Grundy as a 'foreigner.' Very few people live there
who aren't from there. You can't imagine how insular it is" (Ringle,
F4). The mountain hamlet, which never quite measured up to her
mother's social standards, was nonetheless Smith's home, the place
where she attended public school and, wearing a red velvet ribbon,
was Miss Grundy High. She was fascinated by her classmates, even
drawn to them, and yet she was distanced too; she felt burdened by
a sense of guilt and privilege. Her difference was quite visible: her father had the dime store and she always had shoes. The first thing
Smith wrote demonstrates an imagination already seeking to link
wildly disparate worlds. A novel, written on her mother's stationery
in 1952 when Lee Smith was eight years old, was called *Jane Russell
and Adlai Stevenson Go West in a Covered Wagon*.

When the young writer left Grundy, she thought, in that requisite
youthful repudiation of one's past, that it would be forever. She expected to venture forth into an exciting world – a world worth writing about. Yet it was mining her mountain lode that produced her
best work. "It's so exciting," she wrote, "because it's where you first
hear language."[14] She has said repeatedly that it was necessary for
her to get distance, in both time and place, before she could write
about her native region and use its language.

Smith's parents, who shared their daughter's hopes that she would be a writer, decided that she needed more than Grundy's public schools could offer. In 1960, when it came time for her last two years in high school, she was sent by her parents to St. Catherine's in Richmond, a private school providing a finishing-school atmosphere for privileged young women. The teenager experienced, along with a terrible sense of loss, culture shock. Although personally traumatizing, St. Catherine's was intellectually liberating. Despite the fact that the Smith novel that comes closest to describing her St. Catherine's experience, *Something in the Wind* (1971), contains a scathing indictment of the southern upper middle classes, especially the moratorium on direct expression of authentic feeling, Smith received St. Catherine's Distinguished Alumna Award in 1977.

After graduating from St. Catherine's, Smith enrolled at Hollins, a Virginia women's college. The writing program was just what she was looking for. Smith says it kept her from the pretentiousness sometimes associated with art that she shies away from, frightened by seeing "people become parodies of themselves" (Ringle, F4). In so much of academic life, she says, "people become terribly impressed with themselves. But at Hollins, there was this great spirit of play, which, of course, is what creativity is all about. They made you feel like you could do anything" (Ringle, F5). She and friend Annie Dillard were go-go dancers for an all-girl rock band called the Virginia Woolfs, and her American literature class became so enthralled with *Huckleberry Finn* that they built a raft and floated down the Mississippi River. The trip, "like much in life, turned out to be something completely other than we meant for it to be" (Ringle, F4). So irresistible did the "Huckleberry Girls" prove to the media that "by the time we got to New Orleans we were met by the Preservation Hall Jazz Band on a tugboat and the mayor. . . . People were dropping roses out of helicopters. . . . We had become media junkies, with Mark Twain forgotten" (Ringle, F4). For Smith, the river journey was a cautionary lesson, and she has "pointedly shrunk from the sort of book-tour-and-talk-show frenzy through which so many writers trumpet and define themselves in the media age" (Ringle, F4).

Smith describes her creative writing teachers at Hollins as profound influences: Louis Rubin, George Garrett, Richard Dillard, and, in her freshman year, John Alexander Allen. She points to Allen as a particular influence because of his mythic approach to writing. Long before the media craze Allen used Joseph Campbell's *The Hero with a Thousand Faces,* along with an anthology Allen had compiled, as texts. The class studied the quest motif and the mythic journey as devices for plot and shape in fiction writing. Smith's mind, too, was drawn to mythic motifs. An early, unpublished work about a malevolent creative writing teacher is entitled *Children of Cronus,* and while a student at Hollins she wrote a play – a rewrite of Genesis – to entertain Louis Rubin.

Smith is now in demand herself as a teacher of creative writing. Using her own beginnings as an example, she illustrates for her students wrong directions. In her first writing classes at Hollins she "assumed the last thing anybody would want to read about was my hometown, so I picked an exotic location. I wrote about stewardesses in Hawaii. I had never met a stewardess, or been to Hawaii. Of course, it was terrible. Then I decided I should write something with a strong theme. So I wrote about a family whose house burned to the ground on Christmas Eve. When firemen got there, the only thing they recovered was a music box playing 'Silent Night.' In case anybody missed the point, I called the story 'Silent Night' " (Chapel Hill, 1987).

When Smith encountered the work of Eudora Welty in her freshman year at Hollins she realized with a sinking heart that her subject matter was the small-town life of Grundy she thought she had left so far behind. She remembers "quite well" when Miss Welty came her freshman year to receive the Hollins Medal (pers. comm., 1989). It was not just Welty's subject matter that lit a spark, but her mythic treatment of subjects and her sense of literature as passion. "In some of her essays," Smith says, "Welty talks about literature as passion. In one, she tells of being at a college in Mississippi reading a poem and feeling incredible – feeling passion. This matched my own experience in reading and was what I wanted to produce in writing, so that the reader could feel it, too" (pers. comm., 1989).

Smith also encountered Flannery O'Connor, Elizabeth Spencer, and Katherine Anne Porter in her freshman year at Hollins and learned from them that she "could write out of female experience" (pers. comm., 1989). Her sophomore-year introduction to Virginia Woolf proved a fertile encounter. Out of it, Smith began to develop her idea of the artist, of the moment as the work of art, of art as embodied. In that sense, then, someone who gives a birthday party for a child is as much an artist as someone who produces a museum arti-fact. Many of the things women have traditionally done, Woolf taught Smith, may be viewed as art, although society has not necessarily seen it that way. Smith's "But Is It Art? A Lecture on Woman and Cre-ativity" was delivered as the Baylies-Willey Lecture for National Women's History Month at Hollins College on 29 March 1989. Woolf's blessing was her assertion that the truth of the imagination is as important a part of reality as the truth of reason.

Smith spent her junior year at Hollins in France and then in-terned at the *Richmond News Leader.* By the time she had received her A.B. in English in 1967, she had written a novel that earned her six hours of college credit and won one of twelve $3,000 awards from Book-of-the-Month Club to college seniors competing nation-wide. Prior to that she had published several stories in literary mag-azines. Her novel was turned down by Houghton Mifflin, but a sympathetic editor, Shannon Ravenel, wrote her a three-page letter telling her why. Smith rewrote the novel, which was published by Harper & Row in 1968 as *The Last Day the Dogbushes Bloomed.*

Poet James Seay met Smith when he came to Hollins to read from *The Girl in the Black Raincoat.* They married on 17 June 1967. Seay joined the faculty of the University of Alabama, and Smith moved with him to Tuscaloosa. With her $3,000 prize she "bought a refrigerator and got married" (Jessup, H6). She began her second novel, *Something in the Wind,* while working for the *Tuscaloosa News,* first as a reporter and then as feature writer, film critic, and editor of the Sunday magazine. Their first son, Joshua Field Seay, was born in Tuscaloosa on 23 December 1969. When Seay joined the faculty of Vanderbilt University, Smith taught English at Harpeth Hall School in Nashville. She finished *Something in the Wind* "in a race" before the birth of their second son, Turlington Page Seay, on 22 May 1971.[15] That and her third novel, *Fancy Strut* (1973), which used material she gathered covering Tuscaloosa's sesquicentennial celebration, show anxiety over what might be possible in society for an intelligent and creative young woman. In *Fancy Strut* Smith ex-plored stereotypes more blatantly than in any of her other fictions, not out of cynicism but, she explains, as "an attempt to understand them. I was young, and trying to be good, trying to understand. We all were" (pers. comm., 1989).

Smith says that *Fancy Strut* was necessary for her because "it made me feel that the whole world is full of characters" (Jessup, H6). The novel struck a chord, and movie options were purchased by David Susskind. A series of meetings ensued between Smith and Milos Forman in New York and Nashville. Forman proposed to cast Warren Beatty as Buck Fire and Lee Remick as Monica Neighbors. When negotiations with Susskind fell through, Forman filmed *One Flew over the Cuckoo's Nest* (1975) instead. Of this first phase of her writing career, Smith says, "I was in a fever. . . . All I wanted to do was write and read, and I didn't give a damn about publicity or anything like that. I was just lucky. This book came out. I wrote another book, which came out, and then another. I never went to New York. I never actually met any of those people. But then the bottom fell out. Because even though the critics liked the books, they didn't sell anywhere, which was partially my fault, because I wasn't paying any attention to promoting them" (Ringle, F5).

In 1974 Seay accepted an appointment to the creative writing faculty of the University of North Carolina at Chapel Hill. Smith and their sons moved with him, and all four have remained there since, although the marriage ended in 1982. Smith taught English at the Carolina Friends School from 1975 to 1977. In 1977 she began a long association with the Continuing Education creative writing program at Duke University in nearby Durham. From 1978 to 1981 she also became a lecturer in fiction writing at UNC-Chapel Hill.

Smith had been publishing short stories all along, both in popular magazines such as *Redbook* and *Harper's* and in literary magazines such as the *Carolina Quarterly* and the *Black Warrior Review*. In one of them, "Heat Lightning," she returned for the first time to the Appalachian mountain region for setting. "Heat Lightning," like "Tongues of Fire," has speaking in tongues as a motif.[16] Writing this story led her to try her hand at a longer fictive work set in her native mountains. The resultant novel, *Black Mountain Breakdown*, was a watershed for Smith's career in almost every way. She describes it as her first attempt to write about where she came from and to come to terms with her own life. It was not so much the return to the mountain setting that mattered, Smith says, but the return to the language, the mother tongue (pers. comm., 1989). This, however, presented difficulties: "I wanted to write about the mountains, once I had the necessary distance in both time and place – when you're right in it, you can't write about it – but oddly I found language the most important problem. I found that I couldn't write about the mountains without everybody sounding like 'Hee Haw' " (pers. comm., 1989). She found her solution in Tom Wolfe's *The New Journalism*. Writing a piece on Junior Johnson and stock car races, Wolfe solved a similar dilemma by inventing a voice he called "the downstage narrator." She borrowed the idea: "I found, following Wolfe, that I could put the tone and narrative in the voices of the people I was writing about. With that technique, I could use the language without being condescending" (pers. comm., 1989).[17]

Once she had solved her technical problem and written *Black Mountain Breakdown*, Smith encountered barriers of such magnitude that it seemed the book would never see print. In addition to the fact that her first three novels had all lost money for Harper & Row, Smith's editor did not like the main character in *Black Mountain Breakdown* and wanted her to make extensive revisions.[18] Smith held her ground and the novel was turned down. In a 1980 interview she said, "It's a difficult book, but I like it. I don't want to change it. If forty publishers reject it, then I might."[19]

The result was a seven-year drought, a hiatus between "two writing careers" (Hill, 14), during which no Lee Smith novel appeared. In the interim, she was publishing short stories, some of which won national awards, including two O. Henry awards for short fiction and inclusion in Ted Solotaroff's *Best American Short Stories 1978* of a portion of *Black Mountain Breakdown*, which had appeared in the *Carolina Quarterly*.[20]

Despite the awards, Smith experienced deep self-doubt. Fearing that her writing was self-indulgent, she considered going back to school. Instead, Roy Blount, Jr., a friend and fellow southern writer who was just beginning to attract attention in the publishing industry, set Smith up with his agent, Liz Darhansoff, who read *Black Mountain Breakdown* and circulated the manuscript among editors. Rejections kept coming until Darhansoff contacted E. P. Dutton editor Faith Sale, who says that when she moved to G. P. Putnam's Sons from Dutton, she went with the *Black Mountain Breakdown* manuscript under her arm.[21] Smith had found what she needed – an editor who believed in her and who actively edited her. In 1980 Putnam published *Black Mountain Breakdown* to critical acclaim and popular success; the book went into paperback. Smith's persistence had paid off. In 1981 Putnam followed up with a short story collection, *Cakewalk.*

Also in 1981, Smith accepted a full-time creative writing faculty appointment at North Carolina State University in Raleigh, where she has been instrumental in instituting graduate courses in creative writing. Smith, who derives much satisfaction from teaching, is "one of the most popular teachers in the department," says chairman John Bassett. "Whenever she teaches a class, it always fills up the first day of registration" (Jessup, H6).

However personally and professionally difficult *Black Mountain Breakdown* may have been, it was a turning point for Smith the writer. It was the last time she would deal in a novel with the failed development of a girl. The next novel to treat a single female subject, *Fair and Tender Ladies,* would have a mountain woman narrating her own story with a singing, lyrical mountain dialect so evocative and resonant that critics and readers would express the wish that the voice would never stop. Smith had finally seen published the book in which she faced down her demons; she had weathered the long dry spell of seven years without a novel; she had survived the dissolution of her marriage. The inner release of her creative wellspring is testified to by the three novels that followed *Black Mountain Breakdown*: *Oral History, Family Linen* (1985), and *Fair and Tender Ladies.*

Oral History was such a vast improvement over anything Smith had written before that it was hard to believe it was written by the same person. Far more ambitious in structure and scope than any of her first four novels, *Oral History* employs a panoply of eleven voices in telling a multigenerational story of passion, longing, and loss in a mountain family. The novel plumbs the possibilities of language from ancient song to banal trendiness. It is so complex in structure, so evocative in landscape, so masterful in language, so full in characterization – even of male characters, heretofore a weak spot – that critics responded with awe. Christopher Lehmann-Haupt wrote in the *New York Times* that "*Oral History* is such a vast improvement on *Black Mountain Breakdown* that one hesitates to complain. The rural folk that it treats may long ago have been turned into clichés by imitators of William Faulkner, Flannery O'Connor and Eudora Welty, but in *Oral History* Lee Smith brings them back to life again" (Lehmann-Haupt, C21). Jonathan Yardley, writing in the

Washington Post, concluded, "It's the best novel thus far by a writer whose growth has been steady and sure" (Yardley, B8). Frederick Busch, in the *New York Times Book Review*, called the book "nothing less than masterly" and also made comparisons: "Much has been made of Lee Smith's debts to Eudora Welty, Flannery O'Connor and Carson McCullers, and here I am, adding Faulkner to the list. But what finally demands attention are Smith's large talents. This is her own book, set in her own fictive country. She is nothing less than masterly as she starts us out with ghosts and bawdry, then finishes with wild song."[22]

Frances Taliaferro, writing in *Harper's*, called the novel a "portrait of a corner of America that I'm coming to think of as Lee Smith country."[23] In another way, Smith's persistence had paid off. The *New Yorker* had once written her that it would like to publish her if only she would write about a different class of people (pers. comm., 1983). Finally she had learned to write about her people with such style and grace that attention was commanded, her place marked like Faulkner's postage stamp of Yoknapatawpha County. "Your fictional territory is not necessarily your real territory," Smith explains, "and you have to be true to your imagination" (pers. comm., 1989). Thulani Davis, writing in the *Voice Literary Supplement*, echoes other observers that Smith has taken people who have been romanticized and sentimentalized, or stereotyped and trivialized, and made them understandable: "Smith insists that the most devastated landscape has a spiritual underbelly, a legacy even from those who destroyed it. She lets you see her hillbillies both as strangers do and as they see themselves, full of heart and dignity" (Davis, 11).

Finally, in *Oral History*, Smith tapped into the mythic materials that had intrigued her since studying under John Alexander Allen at Hollins. "I was always interested in mythic things," Smith says, "but until I started working the mountain material, I couldn't give women a mythic role" (pers. comm., 1989). The result was spiritual renewal. No longer bound by the stereotypes and banality of *Fancy Strut*, freed from the paralysis of *Black Mountain Breakdown*, she burst into the realm of the quest motif and mythic journey as devices for plot and shape in fiction writing. *Oral History* contains a spiritual journey from Richmond to the mountains, in search of "the very roots of consciousness and belief."[24] *Oral History* brought Smith the

Sir Walter Raleigh Award for Fiction in 1983, and in 1984 she won the North Carolina Award for Fiction. The book was adapted into a play, *Ear Rings*, by Don Baker of Virginia's Lime Kiln Theater, with music by Tommy Thompson of Chapel Hill's Red Clay Ramblers.

On 29 June 1985, Smith married columnist Hal Crowther in Chapel Hill. They had met on Valentine's Day 1982, when both were teaching in Duke's Continuing Education creative writing program. Crowther, a native of upstate New York, says that he "never even expected to know anyone who pronounces fire 'far,' much less marry one."[25] Smith's seventh novel would be dedicated to his daughter, her stepdaughter Amity.

Smith had expressed the fear that she would not be able to match the achievement of *Oral History*, written at an unhappy time in her life: "I knew that I was doing my best writing, but I didn't ever want to feel that way again" (pers. comm., 1989). But marriage to Crowther brought a stability that enabled her to produce a novel that outsold *Oral History* and won equally high praise from both critical and popular audiences. *Family Linen* is a novel of reconciliation, of families breaking up and recombining in a way to make room for everyone. The novel is again set in southwest Virginia and turns on a mystery in a family. Using a real mystery for springboard, Smith plumbed her sense that the family is a mysterious entity. For the first time in her writing career, Smith received an advance large enough to enable her to take a semester off from teaching. In 1987 she won the John Dos Passos Award for Literature, joining former winners John Updike, Graham Greene, and Kurt Vonnegut.

Those critics who had expressed disappointment that *Family Linen* did not measure up to "the myth-laden, haunted lushness of a Black Rock, a Hoot Owl Holler" did not have to wait long.[26] In 1988 *Fair and Tender Ladies* appeared. The consensus was that, in the letters of Ivy Rowe in *Fair and Tender Ladies,* Smith was doing her best work, even surpassing *Oral History.* The seed for the novel was sown when Smith bought a packet of letters for 75 cents at a yard sale and found them to contain a woman's whole life in letters written to her sister. It occurred to Smith that if the writer of the letters "had had a chance to be educated and not have five children, she might have really been a writer of some note" (Ringle, F6). Although critics expressed the opinion that Smith had now gone beyond being a southern writer, the first awards for *Fair and Tender Ladies* came from the Appalachian region. In April of 1989 Smith won both the W. D. Weatherford Award for Appalachian Literature from Berea College and the Appalachian Writers' Award.

By her own admission, Smith used *Fair and Tender Ladies* to prepare herself for her mother's approaching death. She wanted, in her protagonist Ivy Rowe, to imagine a woman with the "guts and grace" to sustain loss, to continue living whole and fully under the crushing weight of life's inevitable, piled-up losses (pers. comm., 1989). Virginia Marshall Smith died in April 1988 of congestive heart failure and complications of emphysema, just after her daughter completed the novel. The most repeated critical comment, in newspaper and magazine articles all over America, was that they never wanted Ivy's voice to stop.

In influencing Bobbie Ann Mason to write what she knew and helping Jill McCorkle to develop her voice, Smith now plays the role Eudora Welty once played for her. Denise Giardina, whose novel *Storming Heaven* is about families caught up in a West Virginia coal miners' armed rebellion, says that when Ivy Rowe tells her daughter in *Fair and Tender Ladies* " 'nobody wants to read about these mountains, honey,' Smith puts her finger on the great wound that cripples Appalachian artists, harms the self-image of mountain people, and allows outside economic forces to rape and pillage the hills. It is the attitude that lets critics dismiss Appalachian fiction as 'regional' and bookstores refuse to stock Appalachian books because, as I was told, 'no one is interested in coal miners.' " Giardina, whose discovery of Smith's fiction was crucial in her development as a writer, goes on to say, "Fortunately, Smith has rejected the warning voices of self-doubt and continues to reveal a beautiful, awful, and misunderstood land to the world."[27]

Smith writes because she is compelled. She writes for self-repair; she writes to release her deepest feelings; she writes for herself. In doing that so well, she writes for the world. All voices are spoken in local dialects, but when they are spoken well they sing a song almost everyone knows.

Chapter Two

Female Experience

We ought not to be awake. It is from this
That a bright red woman will be rising
And, standing in violent golds, will brush her hair.
She will speak thoughtfully the words of a line.

She will think about them not quite able to sing.
Besides, when the sky is so blue, things sing
  themselves,
Even for her, already for her.

  – Wallace Stevens, "Debris of Life and Mind"

One Susan among Many

On 8 April 1969 a little girl named Susan never returned home. She had stopped after school at the house of her best friend who, like Susan, was eight and had long strawberry-colored hair and freckles. A few days later Susan's body was found under a rotting mattress. She had been raped, beaten to death, and thrown out with the trash on a California hillside. In 1989, when her own little girl turned eight, Susan's childhood friend began to remember witnessing the murder. Repressed scenes began to flash in front of her: Susan raped, then savagely beaten, particularly in the head. Finally, she saw the face of the murderer. It was her own father.[1]

  The young woman remembered that her father had told her that no one would believe her if she tried to tell, and that he would have her put away for life if she did not keep silent. Now, with her maturity, her love for her own daughter, and the slow changes in perception wrought by the civil rights and women's liberation movements, she found the courage to come forward and accuse her father of the crime she saw him commit. The days of silence were over.[2]

Lee Smith published her first novel in 1968. It is the story of a girl, two months past age eight, named Susan, who is raped in a game called "Iron Lung." I do not imply that there is a direct link between Smith's novel and the California murder. I am merely pointing to the fact that the writer struggles with the world into which she is born, where there are things in the air she must grasp and understand before she begins to imagine alternatives. Susan was a popular name for baby girls in the 1940s and 1950s, and these Susans were born into a world where such a crime was possible.

The Redheaded Goddess

One of the most fascinating phenomena of the way fiction can work is when writer and audience identify something new and sense, with a feeling of excitement as well as struggle, that they are working on it together. This is one of the places where fiction can do its potentially redemptive work: the work of the imagination at its most creative is to think of a new way to live. Nowhere in contemporary society is this felt as more dramatically and poignantly urgent and necessary than in how females image themselves and society's structures, starting with the most basic of male-female definitions and family structure and going beyond to reimagine what constitutes community and what constitutes the sacred.

The derogation of female flesh in our culture can be, and has been, traced to cultural foundations. For me, the best introduction was Susan Griffin's *Pornography and Silence: Culture's Revenge against Nature*. Equally useful are Elaine Pagels's theological studies *Adam, Eve, and the Serpent* and *The Gnostic Gospels*. Whether we come at it through theology, mythology, or pornography, what is clear is a long story of the tragic loss of an image of sacred, sexual female flesh, a loss that also deprived the male of the joy of sacred, erotic connection. Surveying "myth, religion, and high literature," Paul Friedrich finds the dissociation of sex/sensuousness and maternity/motherliness a barrier against "a more general image of the artistically creative woman" (Friedrich, 182, 190).[3] The separation of these emotional complexes that no doubt derive from the same source prevents a woman from being understood or from understanding herself.

Once the connection is broken, there is nothing left to do but plunder and destroy that from which joy once flowed: the earth, its native inhabitants, its women. This plundering is the most obvious observable truth of Lee Smith's native region. Yet her mother's different origins—as well as the difference of the family's status in town (they were not coal miners, and as a girl Smith always had shoes)—placed her in an interstitial zone, where she was, and was not, of her native land.

The interstitial vantage point via the parents and their position, added to nativity in an already-marginalized geographic zone, placed Smith in the requisite locus to discover the psychological complex that brings together what is usually held as oppositional—the psychological complex that simultaneously affirms emotional antitheses—called by the Greeks Aphrodite. The goddess, in a pre-Aphrodite form as sun or dawn goddess, rises from a pool naked, as goddesses are wont to do, red hair streaming. Here is the naked goddess we have known since the beginning of time.

But Smith got to that vision by a path peculiarly her own, through pristine parlors and mountain fastnesses, before she found her way. Smith says that she writes for self-repair. My guess is that the breakthrough was psychologically necessary, for the cultural grid that made possible the trashing of Susan's mutilated body 20 years earlier in California was still in place in 1989. Just months after the publication of *Fair and Tender Ladies,* the novel in which Smith finally was able to imagine and sustain sacred, sexual female flesh, pop singer Madonna's Pepsi commercial was cancelled because of outrage over her portraying black and female flesh as equally sacred and innocent as white male flesh in her controversial "Like a Prayer" music video.

The message of Madonna's video challenged the foundations of patriarchal culture in its portrayal of sensuous female flesh, in the sanctified domains of the church, touching sacred objects for holy purposes. Madonna's re-vision asserts that female—even *sensuous* female—flesh is equally sacred, equally capable of spilling spiritual blood. This is what jars our well-developed cultural consciences, which so easily associate collective sanctity with males, not females. But in the video Madonna does spiritually—not simply naturally—bleed, and through that experience she becomes involved in a redemptive quest—the search for a sacred. She goes to a jail and identifies the black man in his cell as falsely accused. He is innocent, and she touches him with her redemptive power. The strength that Madonna has gone into a church to gather is strength to do what Susan's childhood friend was required, by love for her own daughter and the pressing of her memory – her whole, undamaged mind – to do: witness, remember, and tell. The neo-Nazi villain who sneers at Madonna in her recollection of the stabbing in the video believes that he has her in his power, that she will not tell what she has witnessed. With his scoffing sneer, he reminds her of what Susan's friend's father had reminded her in order to silence her: her powerlessness, her inability to inspire belief.

They were both wrong. Yet the huge corporation of Pepsi carried through with silencing. Public reaction to the video only served to clarify its meaning: If you do not reverence black and female flesh, you will hurt it. Nor will you trust it, on which Charles Stuart counted later that same year when he murdered his pregnant wife in Boston, knowing the authorities would accept without question his story of a black killer. Both males counted on the white male privilege to inspire belief, but in both video and reality the privilege was abrogated.

What may be most radical about Smith is her valuation of traditional female experience. She places her faith in what seems most unlikely to inspire belief. Partly this springs from her deep antihierarchical stance; she refuses to believe that setting a table is less important than slogging through a battlefield, or that sweeping a floor is less substantial than signing a contract. Further marginalizing her is her embrace of dismissed images of the female as frivolous, dangerous, or both. It is as though her bent is to go directly to the marginalized edge to reclaim; it is oppositional to the chauvinistic impulse, which bases identity on difference and hierarchy. Smith's heroic females are hairdressers, cheerleaders, or disheveled women who bake cakes from scratch. In fact, the most healthy and successful character in *Black Mountain Breakdown*, where the psyche in Crystal, a silenced female, succumbs to paralysis, is a redheaded girl who changes her name from Pauletta to Babe and tapdances through the house wearing her mother's lipstick and pearls.

The fact that Babe is a minor character does not diminish the significance of the detail. While writing *Black Mountain Breakdown* Smith was still unable to imagine fully, as Faulkner never could, the successful active adult female. But the process of renaming[4] is too significant to ignore; its importance is underscored in light of Smith's short story "Saint Paul," in which an ascetic intellectual named Paul, a professor of religion, prefers to fantasize about ideal women, not to hold and touch real women. The name Paul means "little," which makes Pauletta "little little." Babe is not having it; she is not going to be a diminutive of Paul. She chooses for herself a name suggestive of several facets of female sexuality and of the infant stage – starting over, redefining herself. Babe declares that she is going to be an actress, ignoring all the voices that tell her it is impossible. She first goes to New York and makes a fortune in shampoo commercials, then returns to act in the Barter Theater in Abingdon, Virginia, as she has always wanted to do. Making her choices and carrying them out, Babe returns for Crystal's wedding, "awkward, perhaps because she used to idolize Crystal so much. Babe's red hair is long and curly, and makeup rings her eyes. She wears violet stockings beneath her long black skirt."[5]

So Babe is one of the red women, a foreshadowing of Red Emmy in *Oral History*, and this babe is no victim. Nor does her full femininity make her a femme fatale, as cultural conditioning warns and as Crystal fears. Crystal, on the way to self-destruction, "looks at herself in the mirror: messy hair, no makeup, filthy wrinkled dress. The *femme fatale.* She holds up her hand, and the ruby flashes red in the mirror, red as blood in the mirror, holding secrets" (*Black,* 202). Here are two possibilities for redness, in Babe and Crystal. Crystal succumbs to the rigidity of cultural constructs, which would see female, red, and blood in conjunction as negative. Both *Black Mountain Breakdown* and *Fair and Tender Ladies* have preachers named Garnett, uncles to Crystal of the former and Ivy of the latter. The redstone imagery and naming would suggest that condemnation lies in hardening and rigidity. Ivy, the redemptive female protagonist of *Fair and Tender Ladies*, refuses the condemnation, refuses to listen to her uncle when he quotes biblical passages that condemn women. For women must refuse it, as Smith does as she writes her way out of patriarchy. In the novels that follow *Black Mountain Breakdown*, redness is redeemed by female blood.

Chapter Three

Girlhood and Adolescence

Beauty is momentary in the mind--
The fitful tracing of a portal;
But in the flesh it is immortal.

   – Wallace Stevens, "Peter Quince at the Clavier"

The Last Day the Dogbushes Bloomed

In her first novel, *The Last Day the Dogbushes Bloomed,* Lee Smith establishes her direction with the recounting of the pivotal summer of a little girl who has just turned nine. A brief look at this young writer's primer is like surveying an artist's palette. Susan, the novel's protagonist, is struggling to figure out what things are and how they work. All the basics that Smith is going to work with in a long writing career are here: language, naming, color, form and meaning, margins, spirit and matter, nature and culture, experience and authority, sex and death, female identity, definitions of the sacred. All the tools are here for participation in the enormous task of renaming required in a period characterized, in the words of Joseph Campbell, by "rapidly disintegrating systems of belief."[1] Smith's work is part of the demythologizing and remythologizing necessitated by the crumbling of the patriarchy.

Susan lives in an interstitial zone somewhere between the mountains of Smith's paternal ancestors and the shore of her maternal ones. The book is concerned with borders and thresholds. Susan marvels at how her father's basement workroom, closeting his secret paintings, is like being inside and outside at the same time, a liminal quality she also observes of the back porch. Nadine Gordimer asserts that "a writer is a being in whose sensibility is fused what Lukács calls 'the duality of inwardness and outside world' and he must never be asked to sunder this union."[2]

23

Constructed reality is broken by the fantasy figure "Little
Arthur," by a vision of mountain dogs in the moonlight, and by the
possibilities of form and color that haunt Susan's house at night in
the form of a thousand ghosts, a different color for every day of the
week. Limits between self and world are explored when Susan
dreams her thumbnail grows around the world, and men come with
signs reading, "Do not touch this girl. Her fingernail is too long."[3]
(In one of her father's paintings of her mother, the mouth goes "on
and on forever. I knew it was awful but it was beautiful too" [*Last*,
119].) In trying to cope with a world too complicated and cruel to
comprehend, Susan is first drawn to the dominant culture's ordering
principle. For comfort, she breaks words down into spellings, the
component parts of language. She considers cutting her mind up
into boxes, so that she can keep her summer knowledge discrete,
separate. Yet this possibility is rejected by the novel's end, when Susan redeems herself by seeing herself as one with the green world,
even in its dying, even though there comes the last day the dogbushes bloom. Life and death, intermingling and separation, and the
embracing of life's cycles will continue to be themes in Smith's fiction, from Sybill, the confirmed virgin of *Family Linen* who cannot
bear the Peace rose, whose crimson center bleeds into yellow petals,
to Florrie, the heroine of "Cakewalk." The last cake Florrie bakes
from scratch mirrors nature in its autumn leaf shape and icing, each
color flowing into the next.

In the course of the summer, Susan's mother runs off with a
lover, a flood destroys Susan's wading area and sweeps away the
small animals she counted as friends, the family gardener (Frank)
dies, Susan's sister becomes engaged, and Susan is raped. In the tu-
mult of this knowledge, Susan is asking what things are, both in
name and in essence – what sex is, what death is, what love is. She is
exposed to the pornographic mind and patriarchal violence in Eugene, a child visiting from the North who has the children in the club
he forms punch a painting of a nude female. The act forces Susan to
wonder if beauty provokes violence. If so, she is not sure that she
desires beauty. Susan may even wonder whether she wants to be a
woman.

Eugene claims to be accompanied and inspired in his fantasies
by a two-foot-tall figure he calls "Little Arthur." This desiccated version of the Arthur of old wears a "cocked" red hat, has a loaded gun,

and inspires Eugene to invent pornographic games that include, finally, the rape of Susan in a game called "Iron Lung." The idea that there is some sickness with the chivalric ideal, or with a king whose return is awaited, is confirmed by other occurrences of the name Arthur in Smith's fiction. In *Family Linen* Arthur is a dysfunctional brother, a failed rock musician turned alcoholic housesitter. The Arthurian legend's high regard for the female principle has, in this Arthur, devolved into skirt-chasing, which may be either a comment on our puritanical culture's diminution of eros or a withering of the legendary figure. The redheaded father of *Fair and Tender Ladies*, John Arthur, has something wrong with his heart. This plays out in such a way that the mother must shoulder the heaviest burdens and thus becomes embittered. The *rex inutilis* ("useless king") eventually dies, but there is a whiff of eternal return in the birth of an illegitimate grandson whose mother, Beulah, names John Arthur after her father. Beulah's grandmother remarks that when a spirit goes out of the world, another comes to replace it.

Already in this first novel, Smith is dealing with the mythic constraints on male and female locked in patriarchal culture's iron grip and is trying to imagine a way out of them. Susan recognizes that her father, culture's patriarch, is not a king, and she cannot rely on him to provide her a way out of the violence. Nor with her summer's knowledge can she pray any longer to the culture's patriarchal white, long-bearded god. Susan turns instead to the fairy-tale mythological structure that encodes and ennobles nature, sensuality, and female experience. She recognizes her mother, wearing a red so deep it looks purple, as the Queen, and her mother's lover as the Baron. A dark-skinned man she pictures on a black horse, the lover is the first of many liberating dark or borderline figures in Smith's fiction.

The only candidate for king in the novel is even more of a borderline figure, the King Dog of Susan's moonlight vision who transgresses boundaries between transcendent and immanent, between animal and spiritual. Susan's sole use of the epithet "king" reverses patriarchy's sacrifice, whereby Abraham leaves the women behind on the plain and climbs the mountain with either Isaac or Ishmael to encounter the transcendent, male-imaged god outside of nature who will demand the violent death of the animal.[4] In Susan's moonlight vision, 13 wild dogs descend from the mountains to encircle her in a white field. The beautiful King Dog, accompanied by his 12 apostles, brings spiritual renewal. Oppositional categories are simultaneously affirmed as this manifestation of the sacred from the mountaintop comes in animal form. Susan's vision looks forward to *Oral History*, in which renewal comes from the mountains, and to another animal, Whitebear Whittington in *Fair and Tender Ladies*, who lives up on Hell Mountain – "wild, wild" – and runs through the night "with his eyes on fire and no one can take him, yet he will sleep of a day as peaceful as a lullaby" *(Fair,* 315). The conjunction of animal and spiritual is imaged by the sisters Hibbits in *Oral History* as they draw "a bear in the dirt with the point of a stick and then an angel" *(Oral,* 89).

The King Dog is the only king in Susan's fairy tale, and he is beautiful, powerful, and a friend, but the Queen, the adult female, remains the most beautiful and potent figure of all. Along with the cycles of nature, Susan's own nature demands that she ask questions. Who is she? What are the identities of her mother and her sister? Her mother's nature she seems to be most fascinated by, although she does not know if hers is like it. In the novel's opening scene, replete with the floral imagery alluded to by the book's title, Susan plays a word game in which one side of her mouth asks the other a question: "Like I would say, 'Name a red flower,' and the side that said 'rose' first won" *(Last,* 1). In her pink robe with roses, Susan's mother reminds Susan of a butterfly, a red flower, or "anything bright and quick"; her hands are "always moving, fluttering like the birds in the trees beyond our field. . . . They were like those birds, only prettier. I felt very lucky. Not everyone has a Queen, but she was a real Queen all right" *(Last,* 5). Watching a party from her perch on the stairs, Susan sees the Queen as "greener and cloudier than she had been in her chambers" and as a "night sun, glittering and bright" *(Last,* 43).[5] She "looked quiet and still, but she wasn't. She was always moving in small ways, a thousand ways at once, and most of all with her little bird hands" *(Last,* 44). She stands for mobility, "movement that will not be halted."[6]

The Queen is linked to nature and nature's cycles, but those cycles bring bleeding and death as well as life. Susan is confused about the nature of the feminine as she watches her mother preparing to leave home and her sister, Betty, preparing to become engaged to a man her mother says is "a fine, solid, boring citizen. Like a rock, and I quote" *(Last,* 108). Her confusion mounts as to female rituals. "I thought about the first time the Queen had told me about it, about all the blood and everything. She told me that the blood would come and that I would not get scared, that I would wear something to stop the blood when it came. I thought I had to wear a bucket like you play with in the sand. When I told the Queen that she laughed and laughed and one time later I heard her telling a golden lady in the Court what I had said. That was awful, but I guess Queens have the right" (*Last*, 41).

A flood brings death to Susan's wading house animals, but even more confusing is the cat, Anna Karen, who gives birth to a deformed kitten with a hole in its back. When the children pour iodine into the hole, the kitten dies. Gregory, the owner of the cat, tells Susan, "It's named for a Russian lady who got killed when a train ran over her" (*Last*, 9). Susan wonders why the lady did not run when she saw the train coming at her. Burying two dead flowers from her dogbushes (so named by Susan because she found a sick collie lying underneath and nursed it back to health), Susan muses that maybe everything yells when it dies. "Maybe all the grass was yelling right then, when Frank [the gardener who dies] mowed it with the lawn mower; maybe it was yelling help in a million awful voices and I couldn't hear. Maybe the tree hurt when the wind blew it, and cried like it was sick" (*Last*, 9).

Susan thinks she "wouldn't mind it too bad to be under the earth. . . . If I was under the earth I would know everything in the world, and I wouldn't mind it at all" (*Last*, 99). Leonard Rogoff interprets this as a death wish,[7] but Patricia Monaghan is more illuminating: "Then we see that the mother, the lover, and the sister were all aspects of a single grand figure: the queen of heaven, who may have been the life-giving sun itself, as able to parch the earth into a desert as to reclaim vegetation seasonally from beneath the earth's surface" (Monaghan, 150). I am suggesting that Susan also has marks of the goddess.

Caught in cycles of creation and destruction, Susan suggests that the children's club tear up the roses – the flower she links to her mother – of old Mrs. Tate; she says that she does it to prove she is not a silly girl. Shortly thereafter, Susan is raped by Eugene. She wonders

about love a lot and . . . couldn't figure anything out. There are about a zillion things that you call love, and none of them are like each other at all. I loved

John Doe [the stuffed elephant she sleeps with who is always homesick because he misses Africa]. The black man in the art book loved the black woman.
The Queen loved me. God loved the world. I loved Little Arthur. Eugene loved
Little Arthur and I didn't love Eugene, but I loved Little Arthur too. It was all
different. I thought that if any old boy ever told me he loved me I had better
ask him which way, quick, before anything else happened. (*Last*, 110-11)

Here is one statement of the central issue, for the loves are like each
other; the disjunction is false. At the base of Susan's difficulty in
understanding herself, her mother, and the world is the disjunction
between "two emotional complexes, one including sex and sensuousness, the other such things as maternity and motherliness,"
both of which "involve tenderness and intersubjectivity" (Friedrich,
8). Friedrich argues that this disjunction conceals a lover-mother
archetype whose suppression prevents us from understanding female psychology.

The only straight, therefore paradoxical, answers about love Susan gets are from the black maid, Elsie Mae, whose sparkling shoes
she loves. Besides the Queen, Elsie Mae is the only one who sparkles
and shimmers. " 'Oh, law,' said Elsie Mae. 'You don't have to marry
somebody just because of you love them. And you don't have to love
somebody just because of you marry them' "(*Last*, 112). Susan wants
to know what love is like, between men and women, between blacks
and females, between mothers and daughters. Her sister, invoking
hierarchy, tells her that "it's not a good idea to spend so much time
with the help" (*Last*, 117).

In an interesting merger, Smith brings together two forces
against the white-family-as-sanctuary – at least as elaborated in the
southern United States – northern and black, in the name of a minor
character in *Black Mountain Breakdown*.[8] Eugenia Blackman, one
of Crystal's students, writes a spirited if jejeune artistic credo
(perhaps a neophyte Smith artistic credo): " 'If I could have anything
in the world I wanted, it is ESP,' Eugenia Blackman writes in a neat
little back-slanted hand. 'I would like to look into the dark heart of
man. I would like to know what is real and what is made up. I would
like to know if granddaddy thinks at all or just sits there' " (*Black*,
180). Eugenia cannot figure out whether the patriarchy is alive and,
if so, if it is thinking.

All Susan's perplexities can be attributed to the paradoxes inherent in nature and in the disjunctions invoked by society's codes,

such as the hierarchical taboo invoked by her sister's urging her not to spend so much time with the help. The principal, and oldest, disjunction, which, as I've noted, Friedrich asserts is to conceal a lover-mother archetype whose suppression prevents us from understanding female psychology, is at base the source of Susan's difficulty in understanding herself, her mother, and the world around her.

In *The Last Day the Dogbushes Bloomed* – Smith's early exploration into the female psyche – Susan finds healing in language, in naming things directly: "Mother had left us and Betty was engaged and Frank had died" (*Last*, 180). More importantly, Susan recognizes herself, at the end of the summer, as part of the living/dying world: "The roses were all dead now or dying, and Frank was already dead. The wind blew and made me cold, and I thought about the dogs. . . . Frank was like a rock, a tree or a rock, and he was dead. Then while I sat there, that hard green light of dying blew up in me like a flashbulb and I started shaking in my stomach because everything was dying and because then I knew that I was too. I will die; you will die; he, she, it will die" (*Last*, 178-79).

Here Susan begins to pray, although she can no longer pray to the patriarchal god. Like Celie in Alice Walker's *The Color Purple*, she prays to everything; like Celie, she first prays to stars and trees (compare Walker's "Dear God. Dear stars, dear trees, dear sky, dear peoples. Dear Everything. Dear God"[9]):

"Dear star in heaven," I prayed. "Dear star, star, star." That was all I said but I said it over and over through the clear green air straight up to heaven. The star started to move, it danced in the sky, it winked at me and nodded, and the hard thing in my stomach went away.

Next I did a funny thing. I looked down from the star to the tops of the trees and I said, "Dear tops of the trees, dear trees, trees, trees" over and over again until I was praying to the trees and they were talking to me. I laughed and laughed. I sat under the dogbushes with everything green and dying around me in the end of summer and I prayed to the grass and to the flowers and to the rocks and to everything, and everything talked back to me and it was all the same. It didn't matter what I prayed to. (*Last*, 179)

Finally, Susan prays to the wooden steps. (Note that in the progression of things she prays to, Susan literally brings the sacred down to earth.) Going inside, she puts on her new yellow dress and red strapless shoes and goes off to dinner with Daddy. But first she

smiles at Little Arthur, to show him that she is not afraid. The red
shoes, like the red shoe at the end of Alice Walker's *Temple of My
Familiar*, seems to be an external sign of eternal female presence,
and acceptance of the red shoe seems to indicate acceptance of the
feminine way without being excluded from everything else in the
ground of being.[10]

Not until her fifth novel, *Oral History*, would Smith recapture as
whole and satisfying a vision. The novels between *The Last Day the
Dogbushes Bloomed* (1968) and *Oral History* (1983) deal in esca-
lating intensity with social forces that would separate a young
woman from her self. Susan's childhood affords her a freedom to define herself that is not granted to the socially circumscribed debu-
tantes, young wives, and matrons who populate Smith's later novels–novels that follow Smith's own marriage. After Susan, Smith's
women have been taught too well to meet the expectations of others
and screen themselves from themselves. It becomes increasingly
clear how the adults in Susan's family have become emotionally cut
off from their own lives. Smith's vision darkens until the implicit ter-
minus is reached in *Black Mountain Breakdown* when the protagonist succumbs to catatonia.

It may be worthwhile to examine for a moment why Smith's
outlook becomes so bleak. The answer would seem to be that, as she
looked around in society, she saw no possible channels for creative
female intelligence; thus her female protagonists grow older and become more socialized with no possibilities for channeling their creativity. What Smith seemed to see was that, rather than establish
routes for female development, society encouraged females to
remain in a state of arrested development. This is what Crystal's catatonia symbolizes. Society lacked both practices and myths that sanctified female development.[11]

Something in the Wind

Brooke, the 17-year-old protagonist of *Something in the Wind*, does
not find liberation. She longs to find a language of the heart, but instead of turning to wind or water (as the novel's title and her name
imply) she turns to texts–first to *Ripley's Believe It or Not*, then to
the King James Bible–and winds up spouting garbled clichés. The

child of the first novel succeeds better in coming to terms with the life cycle than the adolescent of the second, for whom coming of age means an accommodation to society, which in turn means self-destruction. This observation, conveyed fictionally by Lee Smith, is the same one Carol Gilligan has conveyed analytically – that whereas preadolescent females are full of creativity, confidence, and power in self, adolescent females lose this confidence as they discover the world does not work for them.[12] The theme of self-destruction extends into the next two novels, where female passivity robs the developing female of her will as she allows cultural images to blot out her self. Smith traces the arrested development of the female to its culmination until the protagonist of *Black Mountain Breakdown* lies paralyzed on her childhood bed in her mother's house. Only then is Smith able to break through, construct, and write about a different, larger world that offers women constructive roles.

Something in the Wind opens with what Brooke is reading, a *Ripley's Believe It or Not* anecdote in which a man trades his wife for a valise (compare *Oral History*, in which Almarine trades a mule for Pricey Jane). Brooke reads to kill time on a train bound for the funeral of her best friend, Charles, who has been killed in a car wreck. Charles, she says, "made her mind," a pun we may take both ways. Men continue to make her mind, in both senses of the phrase, as her father cautions her about how to behave at the funeral – "I think you know how to act"[13] – at which the minister sanctimoniously intones, "This is not the hour for mourning" (*Wind*, 15).

Returning to her private girls' school, Brooke finds that her classmates have discovered a "new vocabulary" (*Wind*, 20). They utter distancing, formulaic phrases like "So sorry to hear of your loss" or "So sorry that Charles has passed away" (*Wind*, 20). Brooke feels every force driving to separate her from her self and to falsify her experience. She desperately wishes to stay connected through language, but at every turn she finds human experience suppressed or denied by prescribed language.

Brooke divides herself into an authentic self, which she will keep secret, and a fabricated self, which she will present to others: "I decided to make a life plan. . . . The only concrete thing about the life plan was that it involved imitation. I would imitate everybody until everything became second nature as the song says and I wouldn't have to bother to imitate any more, I would simply *be*" (*Wind*, 22,

25). Thus Brooke colludes in the cultural conspiracy against authenticity.

When Brooke enters the University of North Carolina she seeks out the socially successful to imitate, even though her father's parting clichés have enraged her. Her roommate, Diana, becomes the model. In this pair of names Smith attempts but fails to combine nature and culture, the function of Aphrodite. Neat patterns go askew when Diana, weeping over a letter from home, confesses that her home life is terrible, that her father is an alcoholic. Diana's mythic name is not fully developed, or perhaps Diana is the wrong goddess to invoke. The naming mainly works ironically; this is one of Smith's many pairings of women in which one bears a Greek name (culture) and the other an organic name (nature): Diana and Brooke, Stella and Florrie in "Cakewalk," Sybill and Candy in *Family Linen*. Sometimes the two elements are mixed in one name: Iona Flowers, Justine Poole. Smith gets better at naming her characters as she makes her obsessions more obvious and more complex–that is, as she gets better at naming them.

Brooke watches her public self perform, go through the motions, even have sex–after which she feels "dissociated" (*Wind*, 88)–with no feeling whatsoever but a creeping numbness. Socially, she is succeeding; spiritually, she is starving. All this inevitably ends in disaster. The real Brooke brings Brooke Proper to social disaster, largely through her sexuality. Houston, her fraternity boyfriend, thinks it fine that he is sexually aggressive, but he will not permit her to be. At first she views the relationship as protection. She wears Houston's fraternity pin on the tip of her breast, she says, like an amulet, like garlic to ward off witches. (Surely the imaginative concerns that erupt in *Oral History* are foreshadowed here.) But the protection soon comes to feel like a blockade.

Desperate for some kind of breakthrough, Brooke lets go of cold and rational control of her feelings in a scene where she is literally freezing. She wanders off into the snow and, when Houston finds her, even her language breaks down into the incoherence of emotion: "I reached up and grabbed Houston hard, pulling him down on top of me in the snow. 'Come on,' I said. 'Come on, come on, come on.' There were better words but I couldn't think of them" (*Wind*, 99). Houston rejects her in disgust. In *Oral History* Smith goes much farther in breaking down the structure of language to show the incoherence – the release – of emotion. Friedrich points out that there has been almost no research on the language of love, "largely because of the researchers' own concern with cognition and social structure" (219, 220). He goes on to say that we have almost no record of tender communication between mother and child (and he, of course, would argue that such communication and erotic language are one and the same).[14]

Here Brooke meets Bentley, who confronts sexuality directly. Bentley says, "Let's fuck" (*Wind*, 134). Here is the authentic Other, in relation to whom Brooke has a chance to be herself and to learn what that self is. Bentley is also struggling to be whole, also damaged by the past. He is in flight from an evangelist father who used his son for religious theatrics. (Note the damage done to others by preachers in Smith's fiction. A discarded explanation for Red Emmy's nature reveals that she is the way she is – wild – because she has been sexually and physically abused as a child by the preacher and his wife who adopted her.) Bentley needs Brooke as much as she needs him. When Brooke moves into Bentley's basement apartment she feels "real" (*Wind*, 175) for the first time in her life: "Everything that happened was really happening" (*Wind*, 175). "The main thing," Brooke says, "is that we were so happy" (*Wind*, 175). She thinks that, with Bentley, it might be possible to make up a whole new language for telling the truth. The split between the two Brookes is healed; Bentley's cynicism is healed. When Bentley tells Brooke he loves her she literally falls off a cliff wall into water. It is a fall into wholeness. But neither can handle this love as it deepens, releasing sexuality and aggression. According to Anne Goodwyn Jones, "Brooke and Bentley together struggle with their deepening love and sexuality, and with their accompanying capacities for hatred and violence."[15] Fear of the irrational materializes in their basement apartment, and, on the verge of maturity and understanding, they turn back at the sight of children dancing in a ring. It seems to them a vision of innocence that they have betrayed. In fact, it is they who are betrayed by a false idea of innocence.[16]

Separation from the self in Smith's fiction causes the rupture; it diminishes the human spirit. Part of the separation is caused by false images. Hope ultimately comes with the love that heals the spirit, specifically with sacred sex – sexual love that is also spiritual and brings wholeness. The relationship between Brooke and Bentley is spiritual and seems to release spirits. Part of the haunting is their own inability to confront their love and go forward with it. They are surrounded by people – a group living in the ground-floor apartment above them, people they see socially – who are shallow and promiscuous. Bentley and Brooke are neither shallow nor promiscuous; they are searching. But Brooke cannot break free from the detritus of socially manufactured images. Toward the novel's end she sees Bentley dancing with a girl who is an image of what she does not want to become, and it scares her. "She had high, round breasts like pincushions, that never budged as she danced, doing the same little step over and over, occasionally smiling a fake red smile that scoured the room without settling on any of us" (*Wind*, 224). Here is the pornographic image, whose fake smile reassures that there is no spirit in this flesh.[17]

Brooke leaves Bentley. The tragedy of her departure is that Brooke is intelligent enough to have a dim awareness of the enormity of her self-betrayal. She does not know, finally, how to tell herself or Bentley what is important to her, so what is important to her is lost. Unintegrated, Brooke's gift will doom her to being only an observer. In one of the novel's saddest moments she articulates to herself that her flight from Bentley has sprung from a failure to be true to her own feelings, and she is struck with the knowledge, as from a blow, that one day she will look back and know that she had been happy. Neither Brooke nor Bentley is able to make the crucial passage from innocence to responsibility whole and healed. In terms of the novel, the end of their communication is the end of them. And, all the time, the answer was in the wind.

Chapter Four

Young Marriage and Breakdown

Fancy Strut

The images of women in *Fancy Strut*, in a social schema where the spirit is wounded and imagination denied, are more frightening even than the pornographic image near the end of *Something in the Wind*. Myth itself is prostituted in the bathos of the Sesquicentennial Pageant of Speed, Alabama. *Fancy Strut* is a cynical and disillusioned book; in it there are truly no possibilities for the female protagonists to grow intellectually as they grow older and become more socialized, and the men are equally trapped in images.

Fancy Strut presents a dark view of the human community. The dangers Smith saw ahead for the young Brooke and younger Susan as they grew toward womanhood are delineated in this novel of young marriage. In Speed, society kills women and those "wives kill their husbands, and parents teach murder to their children" (Rogoff, 113). It is spiritual death, a state that seems to be a prerequisite for community life. The way to escape this death, as a comparison with the first two novels reveals, is to actively engage the individual imagination with the world. What is evil, then, about the community of Speed is that, in its rigid conventional codes and its failure to allow room for the individual, it kills the imagination. In Smith's fictive world, not only can there be no self-determination without imagination, but there can be no self.

What other way is there to live? The title answers the question. "Fancy strut" refers to a stylized German goose step that requires troops trained to behave as a unit and not as individuals. It is also the marching step required for the most prestigious competitive category at the Susan Arch Finlay Memorial Marching Contest for majorettes, a matter of no small importance for Speed's ambitious mothers of daughters. This is the way people in Speed–its name itself a pretense–get around without any spiritual sustenance or the imagination to think of a way to get some. Members of the community have versions of the fancy strut with which to fool themselves and others. And what is worse, the characters strut their stuff at the expense of or even through others–particularly through their children, and especially mothers through daughters.

The way in which the past can block imagination is evoked in *Fancy Strut*. Miss Iona Flowers (whose name may be heard as "I own flowers"), the hilarious spinster who fabricates details in her society columns to make events suit her tastes, is an artist figure. Her imagination, however, is detached from reality, hallucinatory and overwrought, lost in visions of a past that never was. Smith confesses affection for this character, based on an actual former society editor for the *Tuscaloosa News* who draped everything with bougainvillea in her wildly fabricated columns. In some hilarious way, Iona Flowers's existence seems to signify that the imagination is still alive, albeit running wild. But the imagined grandeurs of the past are ultimately damaging. The pageant, celebrating the victory of white settlers over Indians, takes place even while the repercussions of the civil rights movement are reaching Speed. At the very time black militants are suing for housing in the Ivory Towers apartment building, a member of one of the old families is again elected pageant queen.

Fancy Strut is based loosely on Smith's coverage, as a reporter for the *Tuscaloosa News*, of the Tuscaloosa, Alabama, sesquicentennial celebration. As the 1960s closed Smith was a young married woman taking her place in society. She no doubt wondered how she would fit in and, given the strength of her imagination, why she would even want to. The questions about what is possible for an intelligent female that were central to the early novels tilt toward fears in *Fancy Strut*. Did accommodation to adult life mean death to the imagination and the self, in exchange for a role? Even the imaginative pattern here, an isosceles triangle whose points are three public places where men handle public life, is rigid and claustrophobic. One of these points is an individual–the paranoid and obsessive Manly Neighbors, sitting at his editor's desk at the newspaper office. Another is the football field and adjacent junior high school gymnasium where pageantry is rehearsed; the third is the Rondo coffee shop, where men with considerable confusion confer about protecting women who in fact are protecting themselves.

Monica Neighbors, Manly's wife, is the *Fancy Strut* character who comes closest to continuing the development of female identity begun in *The Last Day the Dogbushes Bloomed* and continued in *Something in the Wind.* Monica's development has not gone well. Like Susan's sister in *The Last Day the Dogbushes Bloomed*, Monica flees from personal and sexual freedom experienced during a trip to Europe. Wracked by guilt when her plane touches down at Idlewild Airport, she surrenders her newfound freedom as quickly as possible to the first man who offers her security. Relieved of the burden of self-exploration, Monica begins to live out a cardboard caricature of life modeled on an image manufactured by women's magazines.

When the novel opens, as Speed prepares for its 1965 sesquicentennial, Monica is going mad and knows it. She is going mad in just the way Brooke will, having split public and private self. Maintaining her carefully constructed image, Monica relegates whatever artistic talent she may have to repeatedly redecorating the house her husband has built for her and harboring secret fantasies of degrading sexual trysts. On impulse, she conflates these two interests at the novel's end by stealing a banal and sentimental painting called *The Elusive Hummingbird* from the seedy motel where she enacts some of her fantasies and hanging it in her tastefully decorated living room. Her confidence that her husband will never notice sums up the marriage.

Monica is probably what Brooke would be after a few years of a dull marriage, and Monica's imagination is even more detached from the life she is living out. In fact, she must have started farther along than Brooke because there is no indication that she ever fought for herself or struggled to become "real." She makes no attempt to integrate her European experience; she does not try to reconcile her sexual experience with the prescribed southern female persona.

Monica recognizes that she is not connecting with anything. She muses that, when the house seemed ready to be lived in, "suddenly, surprisingly, it had gone dead."[1] Her boredom expresses itself in frustration and rage. She kicks the chintz-covered chaise longue in the bedroom, saying "Speak to me" (*Strut*, 29). She is not getting anything back because she has not put anything of her own self in. By living out socially acceptable, flat images of women she is only manipulating things. Although Manly has been "a perfect husband: courteous, thoughtful, warm, devoted, rich" (*Strut*, 33), Monica has a vague, unsettling feeling that her marriage is moving along under false pretenses. The unbidden thought flashes through her mind, "But I didn't want a goddamn Boy Scout" (*Strut*, 33). When these in- tuitive messages come into her mind she either tells herself she is being unfair or escapes into decadent sexual fantasies, titillating her- self with the thought that Manly would die if he knew what went on in her pretty little head. Toward the novel's end Monica tries to ex- press her sexual passion within her marriage, but it becomes clear that Manly will not receive it, as Houston did not when Brooke tried to pull him to her in the snow.

It is no surprise when, fed up with her boredom and rage, Mon- ica hurts and uses another person. With Buck Fire, the transient manager of the aptly named White Company staging the Sesquicen- tennial Pageant, Monica acts out enough of her fantasies to "store up enough guilt to keep her happy for another twenty years or so" (*Strut*, 267). She fails to notice that he genuinely falls in love with her. His transient status gives her license to indulge herself and to mentally erase him as a human being. The guilt – a recapitulation of the guilt that panicked her when she returned from Europe – seems to bring the permanence she thinks she wants, as she falls back into Manly's arms. She forgets that, in the permanent state, "all was fin- ished and dead" (*Strut*, 29). But death seems to be the preferred state of the community. Perhaps this is part of what Leonard Rogoff means when he says that "the good people of Speed are outcast in their fantasies: their security is too hard-earned, too expensive and too cheap" (Rogoff, 112).

But the fault is not all Monica's. The women in *Fancy Strut* are playing out their allotted role in that patriarchal society. Manly is no help. His name indicates his fancy strut. Manly is one of Smith's will- fully benign men, and by *willfully* benign I mean self-consciously desexed and self-castrated, cut off from their sexuality and aggres- siveness. Manly is an extension of Susan's and Brooke's fathers. He is dedicated to seeing nothing that would jar his Norman Rockwell worldview. This becomes patently clear at the sesquicentennial pic- nic. Monica, however, does see. She sees a little girl bending over in mandatory cuteness for the crowd of adults; her ruffled panties reading "Daddy's Girl" draw approving laughter, especially from Daddy.

Manly wants Monica to fit into a mold and reinforces her tendency to comply. His jealousy of the natural grace of Lloyd Warner – the Ivory Towers suit lawyer who sees too much, who is sick of "all this Faulkner shit," and who is probably closer to the author than any of the other characters – tells us something about Manly: he is afraid to trust himself. He is afraid he will be exposed as not having "natural grace." He can be of no help to Monica because he is as eager for her to maintain her image as he is to maintain his own. Their images are mutually sustaining, and, sadly, there is no essential connection between them.

While Lloyd Warner may appear closer to the author than any of the other characters, it is Sandy DuBois – the shameless hussy – who foreshadows the Aphrodites that emerge as Smith's fiction matures. Sandy's shamelessness is not only an aspect of Aphrodite, but she is also liminal in various ways. Liminality is Aphrodite's most distinguishing characteristic; her function is to transgress borders, making union possible. Aphrodite is the life-giving violator. The name DuBois means "of the woods," foreshadowing the name Silvaney in *Fair and Tender Ladies*. Their names as well as some characteristics link Silvaney and Sandy DuBois to nature rather than to culture, to wildness rather than to domesticity. Sandy is one of Smith's characteristic two-syllable organic names, and as organic matter *sand* may be liminal. Sandy dresses not as a staid puritan but as a wild Indian in the White Company pageant. Furthermore, she bridges domains and characteristics when she decorates her house with angel hair, a spun-glass Christmas ornament, to torment Frances Pitt, the proper managerial wife who is allergic to angel hair. Thus Sandy is that mixture of sacred and profane that Smith gravitates toward and that also characterizes Aphrodite. Because Sandy's sexual charge is positive and Silvaney's negative, Sandy would resemble Aphrodite in her synthesis of nature and culture (Friedrich, 93) whereas Silvaney is just running wild after brain fever. Silvaney, who looks like she was "fotched up on the moon" and runs wild in the woods, may be linked to Artemis. On the other hand, she may reflect the damage done the Aphrodite complex as the dominant culture polarized into puritanism and its inevitable twin, pornography.

Anne Goodwyn Jones has pointed out that Smith's women, usually married, are caught in "a cycle of guilt, self-deprecation, entrapment, rebellion, and again guilt that screens them from themselves"
(Jones 1984, 253). Monica is a clear example of this cycle and
demonstrates that it always leads back to entrapment. She cannot be
direct: her detachment from her own sexuality and aggression forces
her to be manipulative and deceptive, even with herself. She decides
to have a baby – the one form of expression society allows her – and
will go on to reproduce the kind of home from which Susan and
Brooke wished to escape. Fleeing from any kind of self-knowledge,
Monica will use and damage her children. Expressing oneself, including the erotic and violent urges, is hard, but the alternative has a
cost, and that cost is paid by others.

The characters in *Fancy Strut* do harm to others as they posture
and pose. They project their problems outward, avoiding confronta-
tion with the self at all costs. Other people are not really there for
them, except as an audience. That is why the huge, bombastic
pageant of the sesquicentennial, with its faked tradition, is hilarious.
It is an extension of the public lives these people lead anyway, and it
exposes the poverty of their imaginations. The debacle of the
pageant's ending underlines the fact that victory is by defeat. Instead
of being just sad, as in the case of Brooke and Bentley, the self-engi-
neered failures of Speed are, for the reader, tempered with hilarity.
These people are caricatures who seem familiar yet unreal, or at least
they are so fully living out their lives as caricatures of themselves that
we do not care about them as we do about Susan and Brooke.

There are redemptive characters in *Fancy Strut*, notably Lloyd
Warner, Sandy DuBois, whose Indian costume at the pageant inflames poor Bob Pitt, and Sandy's daughter, Sharon, whose bursting-
with-life skin inflames the boy next door, Bevo, as he watches her go
out with her boyfriend, the football star Red Hawkins. In fact, Bevo
mercifully brings the pageant to an end by setting the stadium on fire
to get Sharon's attention. Bevo's oddly Greek-looking name signals a
presence that must be identified. A closer look at the three – Sharon,
Red, and Bevo – reveals a connection to another famous triangle:
Venus, her lover Mars (the red planet), and her enraged husband,
Vulcan (thus the *v* in Bevo's name), the god of fire. And, sure
enough, Red is a warrior/football player, and Bevo's fascination with
fire develops throughout the novel.

Bevo's mother is one of those managerial women who damage their families in Smith's short stories and novels; their malevolence is attributable to the fact that, like the willfully benign males, they are desexed. But his grandmother is a goddess in the third phase (nymph/womanhood/old crone) who grows monstrous vegetables and snorts at danger: "Ruthie said, 'Isn't this fire the wildest thing?' 'This is nothing,' said Mamaw. 'When I was forty I was attacked by a house cat'" (*Strut*, 327). Mamaw knows from experience that domestic life may be more dangerous than anything Bevo can imagine.

Black Mountain Breakdown

Crystal Spangler, the beautiful protagonist of *Black Mountain Breakdown*, stands for Psyche, the soul itself, represented in Greek mythology as a beautiful young girl. Yet hers is ultimately a damaged psyche. Crystal, living in the 1950s and 1960s in Black Rock, Virginia, moves about in a demythologized world, where beauty is trivialized rather than seen as immortal. People respond to her as matter: "Crystal Spangler's pale-haired, fineboned ethereal beauty, her surface, that part of her seen most by others and least by herself, works against her from the moment she's born" (Jones 1984, 261).

In Greek mythology Psyche is figuratively awakened by Eros, as Eros is awakened by her: meaning and passion are mated.[2] It is not simply an encounter; it is a communication. Each erotically awakens the other to learn who the other is. By contrast, Crystal's erotic initiation is a cruel exclusion of meaning, a parody of awakening that puts part of her to sleep.[3] Nothing in Crystal's world shows her how to connect the outside to the inside. In fact, no world could be more split.

Crystal's home is a paradigm for dissociated sensibility. Her manipulative and relentlessly pragmatic mother is all matter; her withdrawn and isolated father is all spirit. Home has been reified: mountain roots have been severed in favor of provincial middle-class pretensions. In the New South of Crystal's mother, Lorene Spangler, French provincial furniture carries the day. Even Crystal's middle name, Renée (French for "reborn" or "born again"), reflects her mother's pretensions, although this does not exhaust its meaning.

Trends have won the day; things have replaced spirit; false sophistication has placed its veneer on human experience.

Crystal's father, who should be teaching her about men and the world, has abandoned the corporeal world insofar as possible. Grant Spangler, scion of a family in decline, has steadily withdrawn from the world into the front parlor. There he courts death, keeping himself numbed with alcohol, cigarettes, and feverish reading. Crystal sits at his feet, chewing the hem of his blue silk robe, as he half-sits, half-lies in his chair and overstimulates her senses by reading "Little Boy Blue," "Abou Ben Adhem,"[4] and "The Spider and the Fly." One of the meanings of the last poem, Crystal's favorite, must be that Grant lures Crystal into his parlor. She loves it there, with its smoke and whiskey smell, the room dimmed by closed blinds and a shirt thrown over the lampshade. It is not a pretty parlor; it is more like an opium den. Grant uses poetry like a drug, to escape rather than seek a deeper engagement with reality or the metaphysical. He wounds Crystal to the extent that he himself is wounded, isolating their experience from the world as he himself is isolated.

Lorene is the quintessential pragmatist; she "ignores everything she can't change" and "deals with her problems by rising above them" (*Black*, 21). Her idea of rising above is to redecorate, a compulsion she shares with Monica of *Fancy Strut*. While Grant gradually withdraws to the front of the house, Lorene gradually withdraws to the back, redecorating the kitchen and putting all her hopes in her beautiful daughter, "the child of her old age, the joy of her heart" (*Black*, 21). Admiring her Florida Rose nail polish, Lorene watches television and thinks self-congratulatory thoughts about how she, like Perry Mason, can figure out "what makes somebody tick" (*Black*, 20). By this metaphor Lorene unconsciously betrays her mechanistic concept of the human spirit. She congratulates herself that she is "no fool, which is a good thing, since she is married to one" (*Black*, 20). Lorene married Grant Spangler because he seemed to her to be something higher. He was a Spangler, a wealthy and influential family until the failure of their Little Emma coal mine, and he was a dreamer. She was irresistibly drawn to him as a foil to her pragmatic nature. But the difference between them and their failure of reconciliation meant that they could never make homes for each other. Now Lorene is irritable over his remove to the parlor, once her best room, because she cannot get in there to vacuum. Smith's spiritually empty characters never suffer; they fret. Lorene's French provincial furniture is falling into disrepair, the sunburst clock has stopped, and the artificial logs have fallen over in the fireplace. Still, she is smug about the fact that she has never complained or talked about Grant's drinking to anyone. Appearances mean everything to Lorene, who confuses form with essence.

With everything so divided at this house, spirit and beauty have no home and home has no beauty or spirit. Or, rather, spirit and beauty are in the home but separated and dying. Spiritual values are too weak; domestic values are too bourgeois, violating mystery and leaving out spirit. Nothing feeds anything else; nothing tempers anything else; nothing is reconciled. Everything splits.

Crystal has in her the potential to reconcile spirit and matter. Her ethereal physical beauty hints at an equally beautiful spirit, which her father reaches out to but has no ability to affirm or direct. Her mother, seeing her baby girl – the prettiest child she had ever seen – has at least given her the "prettiest name she could think of" (*Black*, 21), a name that identifies something about Crystal's essence. Smith gets better and better at naming as she develops as a writer. A crystal has many facets: it can refract light in many different ways. Crystal is also one of the traditional gifts for which brides register, along with china and silver. Finally, it is beautiful, a precious substance, looking forward to the names Smith selects for women in *Oral History:* Dory ("gold" or "gift"), Pricey Jane (*pricey* is common parlance for "expensive"). But *crystal* also evokes coldness and a capacity to splinter. In the Middle Ages it was believed that crystal was ice frozen so hard it could not melt. If Crystal is frozen ice, she would appear to be all form and no spirit, connecting her back to the fundamental problem of modernity. But Crystal is more complicated still. In *Man and His Symbols,* Marie-Louise von Franz writes, "In many dreams the nuclear center, the Self . . . appears as a crystal. The mathematically precise arrangement of a crystal evokes in us the intuitive feeling that even in so-called 'dead' matter, there is a spiritual ordering principle at work. Thus the crystal often symbolically stands for the union of extreme opposites – of matter and spirit."[5] Thus her first name suggests that Crystal has the potential, if not the duty, to bring about the union of extreme opposites – matter and spirit – and form the self. Yet this is specifically what she fails to do. Perhaps it is the difficulty of effecting such a reconciliation in the world in which Crystal finds herself that forces her to abandon the self altogether.

When Crystal is 14 the split between spirit and matter is driven home. During the Christmas vacation of her ninth-grade year she pays one of her regular visits to her father's old homeplace on Dry Fork, where her Great-aunts Nora Green and Grace Green Hibbitts and her Uncle Devere live, along with the many-colored ghosts that also haunted Susan. There are real ghosts there, too, like the family patriarch, mine owner Iradell Spangler, who broke his neck when he crashed his car into the rockface in downtown Black Rock, hitting and paralyzing a young high school teacher as she crossed the street with her groceries. Crystal looks at her reflection by moonlight in the wavy mirror over the old dresser, asking, "Who is it there in the mirror? *Who?*" (*Black*, 41). Although this question will not be answered – the name will not be found – until *Oral History*, the season is a clue. Here we are dealing with another mythology. Christmas celebrates the incarnation, the union of spirit and flesh. Crystal is 33 at the novel's end, the age Christ was when he died on the cross. (Through Crystal the gender reverts to the feminine, for not only is Crystal a Christ figure, as evidenced by the first syllable of her name as well as textual imagery, but Christ is an Inanna figure. Inanna, the Sumerian Queen of Heaven who is the first deity whose name we know, descended to the underworld to plead for the life of her brother/lover. To save him she hung naked on a stake for three days and three nights.) Paralyzed, Crystal lies on her childhood bed in her mother's home, her face turned toward the mountains. Crystal is a sacrificial victim. Her life reenacts the cycle of incarnation ending with the re-severing of the union of spirit and matter that Christ's redemptive death was supposed to have obviated. *Oral History* suggests that the reunion of sexual and sacred is required for redemption.[6]

At this Christmastime Crystal is raped by her Uncle Devere, a mindless act in the worst sense. In a twist that shows the extent to which spirit and matter are separated in the novel, Devere is a mental defective who looks so much like Crystal's father it sometimes makes her "cry to see him" (*Black*, 34). He is a mirror image, brutal and ugly, of Crystal's overspiritualized father. (In fact, his name, like Crystal's middle name, is French and means "of glass," as opposed to the more complex "crystal.") Worst of all, in the act of rape he is mindless matter: he appears totally unaware of what he has done. Crystal buries the rape in her unconscious. No one ever finds out about it.

Years later, touring a psychiatric facility as the wife of an ambitious politician, the 32-year-old Crystal sees a young man, a macroencephalitic, in a crib. His moonface, his soft moans, and particularly his gesture of reaching out his hand to her revive her memory of the rape. She remembers the wrench in her uncle's hand and that he did not seem to see her at all: "He doesn't know, she sees. He doesn't know about it. . . . Something missing. Something missing now" (*Black*, 219). Like the first *Homo habilis* who wields a tool, Devere "holds the wrench in his hand, a strange gesture, jabbing at the air like an experiment" (*Black*, 217). Crystal, on her way to paralysis, is found sitting by the crib holding the mental patient's hand. She will not move, just as she did not move when Devere raped her, just as she would not move from her dead father's side until forced. Crystal slips into catatonia or, in Smith's words, "paralyzes herself" (*Black*, 225).

Devere takes Crystal's body with no cognition, no recognition of who she is (in sharp contrast to Psyche, who lights a lamp to recognize her lover). It is a pornographic act in that her existence as herself is denied. That is the essence of pornography. It is as if she were not there when she is most intensely there. It is her outside that Devere takes, ignoring her inner being. In a strange image, we are told that when Crystal is raped, she experiences the pain as a nail driven up into her head (the nail further underscores symbolism from Christian mythology). At first her head seems the wrong place; the truth of her body is denied. Or perhaps it is the right place, as it is a psychic wound. (Or perhaps they are inseparable.) The outside-inside dichotomy already present in Crystal's world (her mother all material, her father all spiritual) is reified in her body through Devere's act. Sex is a language; here communion is circumvented because no language is spoken. Violence merely inflicts its wounds. Healing will come in *Oral History* when the shimmering Red One – the sexual, active female – appears at Almarine's bedside with her words, "Now do ye know me." They remain in bed together for three days, knowing each other. For now, Crystal remains unknown.

When Crystal returns home after she is raped, she finds her father dead. Crystal's father has been, however pathologically, her only

link to spirit in her home. Crystal clings to this last external link to
the spirit, which she can never find within herself. She has to be
forcibly removed from her dead father's side and sedated. When she
apparently has recovered, a preternatural calmness sets in. She begins to dismantle the identity she has constructed. With no feeling
whatsoever she breaks off with football star Roger Lee Combs, a relationship that had fulfilled her mother's idea of her. She plays a
record, "Love Hurts," and thinks, "No, it doesn't" (*Black*, 88). Her
problem becomes an absence of feeling; Crystal is separated from
herself and from love.

The fact that themes from the earlier novels are here recapitu-
lated and driven to extremes implies that Smith is wrestling in *Black
Mountain Breakdown* with central issues. Two themes are inextri-
cably linked: the difficulty of self-definition for women in a culture
that hinges their self-definition on passivity and the necessity of self-
expression for survival, for connection to the inner self.

At Girls' State Crystal awakens one morning to find herself outside, sleepwalking. She hears a man's voice calling her name and
then remembers that there are no men there. The situation, in which
the protagonist of "Tongues of Fire" also finds herself, can be inter-
preted in several ways. One is that it really is a failure in Crystal. She
could only have become connected with the sacred, the self, and
personal destiny with her voice; she kept hoping for a voice from
outside. The hallucination at Girls' State showed that she could only
imagine the call to destiny as a male voice. She almost recognizes her
own voice: "It wasn't anybody she knows. Not anybody she *really*
knows, that is, even though in a way she knows it as well as she
knows her own" (*Black*, 140). Another question to ask is why
women should not be called by the spirit. The protagonist of
"Tongues of Fire" wants to hear god's call like Joan of Arc; she wants
tongues of fire to descend on her head so that she can burst into ecstatic language. But at a deeper level the woman cannot be called
until she can hear a woman's voice calling her, until women can pos-
sess and can call to destiny.

It is the masculine voice of Mack Stiltner, a boy from the hollers,
that Crystal should listen to and answer, as eros tells her. Although
Mack, with his bad teeth, seems the unlikeliest choice, he is the one
Crystal is drawn to sexually. With him she can express her sexuality
openly. Mack is an authentic artist; he winds up in Nashville as a

successful country singer. While they are together Mack writes a song about Crystal that reveals that he sees and understands her. The song, which starts out telling of Crystal's "angel face, angel hair," ends "But angel hair is sharp as glass / You can never get even close" (*Black*, 100). Mack sees that Crystal, like her Uncle Devere, has a side that is in some way dangerous, potentially cruel. Yet he embraces her and loves that in her; he sees a union of spirit and flesh in her. The tragedy is that she, in fleeing from him, occludes that opportunity for becoming reconciled to herself. Like Brooke, Crystal cannot face self-knowledge: "Stop singing that song," she says angrily, "It makes me sound awful" (*Black*, 100-101). When Mack's song exposes that Crystal will let no one come close to her, she wishes she were back with Roger Lee Combs. That was easier; distance made the relationship possible. Lacking the imagination to write songs or find a window into Crystal's soul, the shallow football player did nothing more challenging than give her rings, yoking to himself her outside but not her inside: "Crystal wishes for a minute that [Mack] was Roger, who could never write a song in the first place, but if he did would never write a song like that. All Roger ever did was give her rings" (*Black*, 101).

Mack asks Crystal to come to Nashville with him, saying they belong together and are two of a kind, whether she knows it or not. At the door to psychic maturity, like Brooke with Bentley, Crystal turns back. "We are not," she counters. "You can't have it all," Mack says in a violent outburst. "You've got to decide sometime what you want" (*Black*, 102). But this is precisely what Crystal cannot do. Ultimately, she will let other people tell her what she wants. Like Brooke, she lacks the courage for relationship, with its requisite honesty and self-confrontation. She cannot trust the voice inside her, the insistence of eros, that tells her what she belongs to.

For a moment Crystal hears the sensual and spiritual voices inside her that move her toward Mack Stiltner, but she fails to listen. She lacks the courage to follow her inner guidance. Mack is the Other through whom she could have known herself and another person. Crystal tries all the standard initiation devices and rebellions, all the ready-made roles and identities, but none leads to her innermost self. Unwilling to know and be known, she turns away from what Hannah Arendt calls the "supreme confirmation of one's existence which only love, mutual love, can give."

Crystal never has another chance at what she had with Mack Stiltner. The closest she comes is in teaching. This must be part of the solution; she needs to embrace both eros and her intelligence in order to be whole, but she refuses each by keeping them separate: "The scenes in her classroom show an incredibly different Crystal: she speaks, thinks, chooses, enacts, and has probably more *words* here than in the rest of the novel. Nor should this be a surprise. . . . As a high school student, Crystal loved to go to the blackboard and diagram compound-complex sentences. Patterns, again, and a voice: this is as close as Crystal will come to becoming a Lee Smith artist" (Jones 1984, 262).

Crystal chooses to silence the voices inside her for the security of marriage to Roger Lee, and finally, at the novel's end, she will no longer talk. Any analysis of the factors that lead Crystal to her catatonic state upon the bed in her childhood room does not obscure one important fact: it is ultimately her decision. Smith makes this perfectly clear through language. She does not say, "Crystal becomes a catatonic." She says, "Crystal paralyzes herself " (*Black*, 225).

Crystal could have acted in her own behalf. But, unlike Susan, she cannot verbalize reality. She cannot say "Devere raped me," even to herself. As Smith's characters move from childhood into adolescence and womanhood, they are unable to reconcile spirit with flesh, resulting in a paralyzing split. Smith's own artistic drive searches for that place – in art, in language, in self-assertion, in imagination, in passion – where wholeness lies.

Crystal's student Eugenia Blackman has a name that conflates races, sexes, and even includes the rapist Eugene from *The Last Day the Dogbushes Bloomed*. Eugenia writes a spirited paper in which she wishes for ESP, saying she "would like to know what is going to happen in the future so that if I didn't like it, I could just stay home that day. But I would not be stingy; and use my gift for peace in the world" (*Black*, 180). Crystal compares Eugenia's paper to the one story she had typed for her bohemian lover, Jerold Kukafka, who "said he was probably doing the most significant work in contemporary literature" until he hanged himself (*Black*, 180). His story, "The Puppy," is a bald statement of the problem – that the life women give, which is the only life we have, always has, as its end, death. This makes woman the life-giver also woman the death-dealer, the rub. Smith uses her characteristic humor here to distract the reader from seeing that this is, in fact, the serious – the almost unspeakable – issue on which we have elaborated a whole culture:

> Now she smiles, thinking that the puppy was not nearly as interesting as Eugenia Blackman's desire for ESP. As she remembers it, the only character in "The Puppy" was the puppy himself, left alone on a four-lane highway to die. The puppy tried to cross the highway and was run down, eventually, by a milk truck. "The Puppy" was symbolic, Jerold had explained, an existential parable about a lost soul in modern America, killed in the end by that which seems to nourish. It's the bitch/mother image, he said. But apparently no one could understand it; it was rejected again and again. Editors called for plot and narrative, conventions which Jerold had outgrown. (*Black*, 181)

At the end of *Black Mountain Breakdown*, then, Crystal Spangler, her name suggesting something glittering and shining, lies catatonic on her childhood bed in her mother's house, her head turned toward the window with its view of the mountains. With the parallels between the catatonic Crystal and Christ at his crucifixion, Smith may be suggesting that the way women are crucified is through this failure of development. There is no way for Crystal to develop, no way for her to grow. She has tried every community-validated path to female identity and all end in paralysis. She has tried to pry something from the past, obsessively reading the journal of a female ancestor, who describes how her older brothers dressed her up in their clothes. Never trusting her own voice, she has begged for stories from others – stories of the old days, what the mountains were like then, the forests. What is Crystal looking for in the past? What has been lost? What is the "something missing now"? She calls her friend Agnes shortly before she slips into catatonia to ask if Agnes remembers what song Jubal Thacker used to play on his guitar every night when it was time to go in (*Black*, 213). Agnes does not remember that the song Jubal Thacker played "soft and a little bit sad in the green June night across all the back yards" was the mountain ballad "Wildwood Flower" (*Black*, 13).

It is to the lost past that Lee Smith turns, in her next novel, *Oral History*, seeking a vision of wholeness in adulthood. She finds a place and time where spirit and flesh, mind and world, language and thought, are not divided, and where domesticity includes wildness and passion. She hears the ancient mountain song and lets the healing images emerge, from her own unconscious and from the mythic past.

There is a very important passage near the end of *Black Mountain Breakdown* worth noting. Crystal, for public relations purposes during her husband's political campaign, visits the psychiatric facility (she had thought she was visiting a *pediatric* facility) where she will confront the moonfaced encephalitic who precipitates her catatonia. When she learns that she is to meet a psychiatrist rather than a pediatrician, she is upset. Her secretary assures her that "he'll be trying to make a good impression like everybody else" (*Black*, 215). " 'Dr. John Ripley,' Crystal repeats. It's awfully important to get their names right" (*Black*, 215). At the opening of *Something in the Wind* Brooke is reading *Ripley's Believe It or Not*, so it is curious that the psychiatrist's name is Ripley. And who are "they," the ones whose names you have to get right?

Dr. Ripley, a tall man with a northern accent, tells Crystal the sane are not so different from the insane: "There is a very fine line here. In fact, we have a great deal to learn from the insane. Insanity, Dr. Ripley feels, is largely societal. Or perhaps *situational* is the better word. What we are trying to do is change the situation, break the pattern, teach different behaviors. This is where the new recreational building comes in, he adds. How can we help people learn to react to society in a new way if we have no model of society for them to practice with?" (*Black*, 216).

Using the model of fiction for practice, Smith gets the names right in her next novel, *Oral History*. And she gets them right the way she does everything: by ear. She gets them right by the way they sound, and, as becomes evident in *Oral History*, what they mean, historically, is the revelation. But first the sound.

Chapter Five

Mythic Roles for Women:
Oral History

Unchained Melody, Ancient Song

Facing down her demon, passivity, in *Black Mountain Breakdown* freed Smith to search imaginatively for active images of women. She found them in the mythic past, and her rendering gives those images voice and life, offering women a collective mechanism for psychic renewal in listening to, telling, and re-creating myths. In *Oral History*, her first fully successful fiction, Smith not only outlines a history of the psychic damage that leads to the pain her modern characters suffer, but she offers a means of release. *Oral History* is a tragedy, but a redemptive one. In this return to her own childhood, Smith works back toward the childhood of the human race. "I was always interested in mythic things," she says, "but until I started working the mountain material, I couldn't give women a mythic role" (pers. comm., 1989).

In a lecture at the University of North Carolina at Chapel Hill in 1987, Smith said that *Oral History* evolved from notes and tape recordings she had collected for years – memories and stories compiled from kith and kin in her native southwestern Virginia mountains: "My closets were stuffed with shoeboxes spilling over with this material, and I finally decided I had to find a place to put it" (Lecture, 1987). She wrote *Oral History* as a chronicle of the loss she witnessed personally and also knew from family stories in her land of origin: the loss of a wild and beautiful landscape with great forests teeming with wildlife, even panthers and bears, to the relentless demands of American industry – first lumbering, then railroads, then coal mining; the loss of the native dialect of an oral culture of

great antiquity–fully nuanced, rhythmic and poetic, a language of
the heart–to contact with trendy and banal American mainstream
speech, through radio and television and other kinds of exposure;
the demoralizing of a once proud, independent and self-sufficient
people, brought by economic and societal changes to a degraded
welfare state, through "no fault of their own."[1]

But in singing the ancient songs, in chronicling the familiar loss,
Smith dug up something of far more importance to the damaged
women of her fiction, for she sang into being archetypes whose stories flesh out a mythico-religious history of our species. The chronicling sings an ancient song of the sorrows of woman that tells the
story of her fall from sacred naked goddess–humanity's first religious icon (ca. 40,000 to 25,000 B.C.)[2]–to the whore of Babylon or
the desexualized virgin (Friedrich, 3). One traveler in *Oral History*
says that his journey to the Appalachian mountains is a search for the
"very roots of consciousness and belief" (*Oral*, 97), and this is in
fact the quest of this novel.

The search is crucial. All people need myths to legitimize their
existence–ennobled stories that make conscious and collective,
hence accessible, visions of reality that inspire. Some mythic visions
make the nitty-gritty of life tolerable. Others carry the catalyst for
change by keeping alternative visions present and alive. Many do
both. Western women are particularly in need of these myths, particularly in need of collective, ennobled visions of the sacred, sexual,
and powerful females among us, because that female has been so
systematically expunged from Western history (Combs-Schilling, 255-
71).[3]

Smith discarded some hundred pages of introductory narrative
to *Oral History* when she realized that, against standard English, her
mountain speakers sounded like ignorant hicks (Lecture, 1987). That
was the last thing she wanted. She replaced the discarded introduction with a frame story in which Jennifer Bingham – "a representative
of the modern American class, self-confident yet sheltered, with only
a superficial interest in history or tradition, and deeply naive about
human nature" (Jennings, 11) – comes to the southwestern Virginia
mountain community of Hoot Owl Holler in search of her roots.
Jennifer's curiosity is superficial; she is infatuated with her oral history professor, Dr. Bernie Ripman, "a Yankee from Miami," and

hopes to impress him with research on her family history for her class project.

Smith says she is not sure if her critics and audience understood that the voices that unroll within the story are meant to be what is recorded on the tape recorder that Jennifer leaves at sunset, a liminal state, in the haunted Cantrell homeplace. What is certain is that after Jennifer's self-consciousness and condescension, her hopelessly inflated freshman diction, the voices of the Cantrell past, whose beliefs and values Jennifer's stepmother hoots derisively at over the bridge table, explode with dignity, authority, and force.

The Evidence on the Tape

At the opening of *Oral History* we seem trapped once more in the banality of Smith's contemporary South with the concomitant limitations of her banal narrators. But when the wind – the wind with "voices in it, and thunder coming" (*Oral,* 24) – moves upon the waters, calling spirits from the vasty deep, we step into the mythic past. We gain access to this past through the conveyance of a tape recorder, going back through four generations of the Cantrell family. Three major narrators – Granny Younger, Richard Burlage, and Sally Wade – tell the stories of Hoot Owl Holler, ringed by three mountains, and the tragic life of the progenitor of the family, Almarine Cantrell, born in 1876, the middle of three sons of parents who reputedly came from Ireland, and his fateful matings with three women. The repetition of the number three is significant.[4] Hunting one day on the "wild side" of Snowman mountain, Almarine sees a beautiful woman rising from a pool, naked at her bath. She is nearly as tall as Almarine, her red hair hangs to her waist, and as she turns he sees her mouth like a red slash and the red nipples of her breasts. The sight "sets a stamp on the rest of his life" (*Oral,* 43). She disappears into the mountains, only to reappear at his bed one night. As she lies down beside him, she says, "Now do ye know me" (*Oral,* 48).

Local gossip would turn this wondrous woman into an evil one. Too far outside its stereotypical paradigms, the community brands her as a 40-year-old witch, Red Emmy, who lives with her father, Isom, under the Raven Cliffs. Apparently she has no mother. Society

rumors that she throws her father to his death off one of the cliffs before she moves in with Almarine. When Almarine begins to waste
away, the "wise" old woman telling this part of the tale, Granny
Younger, advises him that the witch is riding him at night and that he
must kick her out. Granny Younger demands that he reinvoke the patriarchal religion to rid himself of Red Emmy, by uttering the names
of the Father, Son, and Holy Ghost. If that does not work, he is to
cut her. Almarine sobs – he is in love with Red Emmy and she is
pregnant – but he follows conventional wisdom. Rumor has it that
she goes wild, runs the mountains, and throws her babe into the fire
after suckling it at her breast for three days. Some say Almarine kills
Emmy, others that she has been seen "whoring" on the streets of
Williamson, and "she looked pretty good" (*Oral*, 91).

Almarine's next love is Pricey Jane. Physically, she is the opposite
of Red Emmy; she is young, dark, and tiny. But, like Red Emmy, she
is enormously appealing and has misty origins. Dark is ennobled. She
arrives on a wagon with gypsies, and Almarine trades a mule for her.
She wears a mysterious pair of earrings – roses traced in gold around
gold loops (the roses that stand for the woman in Smith's fiction) – and her voice reminds Almarine "somehow of a dove" (*Oral*,
59). An enraged old maid insists that the couple be officially married
because that is the way things are done "in this town . . . in this day
and age" (*Oral*, 62). She drags the couple off for an official cere-
mony performed by her brother, a blind old judge lying in a dark-
ened room (here dark stands for the inability to see, not for color).
Almarine and Pricey Jane live in idyllic happiness. She never leaves
the holler ringed by three mountains: "Almarine brings it all back"
(*Oral*, 70). They have a son, Eli, and, at the end of Granny Younger's
narrative, a daughter. Granny, who delivers the baby, tells them to
name her Dory: "Hit means gold" (*Oral*, 68). But one night when
Almarine stays away playing poker, their cow wanders into a patch of
shady wet grass and gets "dew poison" (*Oral*, 78). Pricey Jane and
Eli drink the milk and die. The community whispers that it is
witchcraft, the work of Red Emmy, and that the holler is haunted.
The passion and magic of his first two loves gone, Almarine appears
in later years as the "angel of death himself" (*Oral*, 127); "what was
sharp and vital once, has grown hard and cold" (*Oral*, 93), softening
only when he looks at Dory.

Thinking "a man's got to have him some sons" (*Oral,* 93), Almarine beds down with Vashti, the dark "half-breed" (*Oral,* 86) widow
of his brother Riley who shows up at his door with her daughter, Ora
Mae. Half-breeds in Smith's fiction are liminal figures, therefore en-
abling and potentially potent in Smith's world. Often they are capable of, or inspire, truth and passion missing in the light-skinned. But
here Vashti and Ora Mae eclipse Dory, and one sees the intrinsic
racism available in cultural imaging.[5] Nonetheless, dark figures in
Smith's fiction generally stand for entrances into a more passionate
world. They are seers and survivors. The golden Dory inherits her
mother's golden rose earrings along with the potent female force imaged in Red Emmy, the shimmering Red One who arose from the waters, and in the dark and powerful Pricey Jane.

The longest section of *Oral History* is "Richard Burlage: His
Journal, Fall 1923." As Richard is a representative of Richmond and
of literate culture, his section is written, not oral. Here is the show-
down between Richmond and the mountains, between writing and
the spoken word. Disaffected with the values of his class and dispir-
ited, Burlage decides on a pilgrimage to the mountains, a spiritual
quest. Richard's brother, Victor, who "lost his soul in the war . . .
somewhere in France, no doubt, along with his leg," is described as
a "disembodied voice in the library" (*Oral,* 97). In Richard and Victor "we watch stiff, Latinate, educated Victorian male minds experience essentially abstract and intellectual, white, masculine, post-
World War I angst" (Jones 1984, 268).

When Burlage journeys from Richmond to the mountains seeking "the very roots of consciousness and belief" (*Oral,* 98), he finds
in Dory "all the grace I ever hope to see" (*Oral,* 156). It is Dory who
comes to Richard at the schoolhouse where he teaches, crossing water unhurt (an aspect of Aphrodite) on a swaying, perilous bridge in
a flood (*Oral,* 144) and baring her breasts to him, as does Red Emmy
to Almarine. Dory is beauty, power, action, knowledge of self, and
sexuality. She amazes him with her directness, a far cry from the co-
quettish Richmond socialites he has known. "I understood her desire to be a kind of purity," he writes. "Everything is transparent with
her. When she's hurt, or worried, she cries. When she's happy, she
laughs. When she wants a man, she . . . " (*Oral,* 147; Smith's el-
lipses).

His tightly controlled language breaks down into the "wordlessness of love and the incoherence of immediacy" (Jones 1984, 249). Like Almarine and Red Emmy, he and Dory are "almost exactly the same size, toe to toe" (*Oral*, 155). Equality reigns here, as it did in the distant past, with the shimmering Red One. In this relationship, senses and intellect merge:

> My intellect *trembles with my body* as I consider, again and again, that kiss. (*Oral*, 135)
>> *Bringing me to my senses!* For this is exactly what she has done. (*Oral*, 156)
>> *I don't care.* For once I am living my life rather than watching it pass in review. (*Oral*, 154)

But Richard does not have the courage to sustain the relationship: he imagines the "snide smirk" in his cynical brother Victor's eyes (*Oral*, 147) and returns to Richmond to marry the socially correct Episcopal bishop's daughter. His one attempt to send a note to Dory by Ora Mae is half-hearted. He abandons Dory not knowing that she is pregnant, carrying his twin daughters, Maggie and Pearl, two more golden girls. Dory marries the lame Little Luther and has two more children, Sally and Lewis Ray, but she keeps looking up the railroad track where Richard left and one day lays her head on the spur line and lets the train cut it off.

Sally finishes the Cantrell family saga, telling how the flawed Pearl, last inheritor of the golden rose earrings, leaves her upholsterer husband in Abingdon to run off with one of her high school students who "looks like a Greek god" (*Oral*, 272), telling him in Howard Johnson's that he "really ought to order some vegetables. You know you're a growing boy" (*Oral*, 273). Pearl dies mysteriously after bearing a child, who also dies, and the high school boy, crazed with grief and perhaps jealousy, shoots Pearl's cousin Billy (there is a lurking question of incest). Billy's mother, the perfidious Ora Mae, withholds from Dory Richard's note and throws the earrings into the gorge "that the wind rose from" (*Oral*, 88) near the burial ground. Ora Mae contemplated the power, beauty, and mystery of the full female amongst her people, and then she threw that possibility away. Like Vashti supplanting Emmy and Pricey Jane, Ora Mae starts sleeping with Little Luther after Dory dies and bears him the second Almarine, born in 1940.

This is the family that Jennifer, daughter of Pearl and the upholsterer, finds when she comes to research her family roots in Hoot
Owl Holler. She believes that Ora Mae is her grandmother and Little
Luther her grandfather; in truth, she is no relation to either. The
second Almarine makes a "killing in AmWay" (*Oral,* 285). In the demythologized world of the "American way" (the derivation of
AmWay), even gemstones lose all essence; they mark the steps in
selling success. Al's wife, Debra, wears a T-shirt with "Foxy Lady"
written on it in silver glitter and paints her daughter's fingernails silver while Almarine, who always carries a calculator, installs orange
shag carpet on the floor and up the sides of his van. Finally, "never
one to stand in the way of progress" (*Oral,* 3), he develops the
haunted holler into a successful theme park called Ghostland where
tourists pay $4.50 to see the haunted rocker careen wildly back and
forth at sunset.

Truer than True: Border Crossings

Oral History is obviously about loss and damage. Granny Younger
says the story she tells is "truer than true" (*Oral,* 37). Because she is
representative of oral culture, "truer than true" may mean truth alive
in the oral tradition that is shut out by the recorded "facts" of the
historical tradition. Those facts are privileged, selectively chosen and
disseminated (i.e., controlled), and *recorded* by the dominant culture. Granny offers an alternative view, using her knowledge of human life as evidence. She has, she says, seen folks come and seen
folks go, birthed babies, and buried "many a soul" (*Oral,* 37). She
knows more than the reader, she says – perhaps even more than the
reader wants to hear. Her voice, for that reason, is the voice usually
silenced. What she says comes from long witness; it is cyclical, mythi-
cal truth of which she speaks.

Even Richard Burlage, the myopic man from Richmond – the
"rich world" – gets a glimmer of Granny's home truths when a mountain man says, "I don't want nothing you've got," and then shoots
out the rear-view mirror of Richard's obscenely fancy car (*Oral,*
232). Driving back to Richmond, dazzled by the noonday sun in his
splintered rear-view mirror, Richard feels as he did when he learned
that a ninth planet had been found revolving around the sun, a

planet that–like the "New World" when Columbus "discovered" it–*"had been there* all along" (*Oral*, 234; Richard's italics).

Recording is not the same thing as creating; Richard has an insight into cyclical, eternal truth. Rather than seeing some line of progress, the past discarded, he realizes that everything that ever happened is still happening: "Nothing is ever over, nothing is ever ended, and worlds open up within the world we know" (*Oral*, 234). It is emotional contact with Dory–herself a dazzling light–that makes it possible for Richard to break through, out of his constructed world, at all.

Myth is "basically about emotion," and one way to get at "the emotional wellsprings" is "through the vivid imagery of the texts themselves" (Friedrich, 7). Because fiction works this way as well, we can uncover the mythic centers of *Oral History*–Red Emmy, the first Almarine, Pricey Jane, Vashti, and Dory–through the vivid imagery of the text itself. The novel's surface is so compelling, however, that it requires a wrench of attention to look way from manifest to latent content. The job requires piecing back together the splintered rear-view mirror, repairing the damage, to see what has been left behind.

The earliest stories from the past as the tape unwinds are told by Granny Younger, the Hoot Owl Holler storyteller. It is important that there is a woman storyteller. But her very ability to achieve that role should make us somewhat suspicious of her; she can be the narrator because at heart she colludes with the patriarchy. For the story of the sacred and sexual Red one, she is unreliable. (It is Granny Younger who says of Red Emmy, "You know a woman orter bind up her hair" [*Oral*, 41].) Granny Younger's name implies a bridging of opposites, as does "oral history." A reversal of full cycle, her name implies eternal return. That her voice is heard through the conveyance of modern technology, a tape recorder, is another analog of wholeness that breaks the barrier between past and present.

The story Granny tells is not only truer than true but also "blood on the moon" (*Oral*, 37), linking human life–with its stain–to the bodies and cycles of the cosmos itself. Spatiotemporal barriers are being crossed. The first thing she tells us about Almarine Cantrell is that he is "not but twenty-two years old" (*Oral*, 27), placing us in 1898, just before the turn of the century, another border crossing. Moreover, Granny goes on to say, "Young, then–you could call him young for owning this much land and that's a fact, but they's other ways Almarine is not young now and never was young atall" (*Oral*, 27). Granny Younger, then, is not the only character who is both young and old. Later in her story, when Granny spies Almarine and Red Emmy in the middle of their half-plowed field kissing in the first early spring thunderstorm, she, too, becomes sexually aroused. As the inflamed couple, still holding on tightly to each other, starts across the field toward their cabin, Granny thinks she sees Red Emmy turn her way and spit: "The lightning flashes right then and I see her face and it is old, old. It is older and meanern time" (*Oral*, 52).

Emmy, too, is both young and old. Some of the mountaineers even whisper that Emmy and her father, Isom, are "moren a hundred years old, or old as the hills or older" (*Oral*, 47). Despite her collusion in – or even initiation of – Red Emmy's exile, Granny recognizes her centrality: "Lord Yes, it's that redheaded Emmy's story. Mought be it's her story moren the rest" (*Oral*, 37). Older than the hills, older than time, in what is really her story, Red Emmy is an eternal presence, carrying both sexual passion and murderous rage, both blessing and curse. When she is driven from the community, deemed unfit to be domesticated, she is also carrying a baby.

Red Emmy

Almarine and Red Emmy, as well as being cyclic, are larger than life. He is bigger than the other denizens of the mountain peaks and hollows, and Red Emmy is "as big as he was, a woman nearabout six feet tall" (*Oral*, 44). They are mythic figures, a match, but what mythic figures? In his study of the meaning of Aphrodite, Friedrich examines such forebears of the goddess of sexually passionate love as the earliest sun and dawn goddesses. Ushas, the Vedic goddess of dawn (the Indic rendering for the constellation of female that becomes for the Greeks Aphrodite), for example, is described as surrounded by rays that are "red, purple, ruddy, or red-tinted" (Friedrich, 37). When Almarine comes upon Emmy from the back, "She was naked from the waist up. Her black skirt was pulled down around her hips and her shirtwaist was throwed on the ground. The skin of her back showed the whitest white that Almarine ever seed, and her hair fell all down her back to her waist. And that hair! Lord it was the reddest red, a red so dark it was nigh to purple, red like the

leaves on the dogwood tree in the fall" (*Oral*, 43). The red so dark
that it was purple takes us back to the full female that the preadolescent Susan saw in her mother the Queen but could not envision being. Smith is showing the postadolescent female how to be that
Queen.

Because society charges the figure of Red Emmy with so much
ambiguity, it is important here to look at the ambiguity these sexually
charged sacred females have held through much of time. Friedrich
explains that the dawn goddess "is always young, continuously reborn, and in this sense immortal. She brings the light of each day,
and the powers of that, to man" (Friedrich, 39). But her ambiguity
emerges in that "she also dies every day and shortens and wastes
away life" (Friedrich, 39). This ambivalence is seen in the need to
tarnish Red Emmy's sexuality, whom society reports at past 50 to be
"whoring" in Williamson and still looking "pretty good" (*Oral*, 91).
Red Emmy captures society's hostility toward sexually attractive, wise
women – especially those who are sexually attractive when they are
older.

Red Emmy has many mythic foremothers. Ushas is, for example,
the proto-Baltic Sun Maiden, Saule, who "journeys through the sky
drawn by tireless red horses" (Friedrich, 35). We think of the unsat-
isfied modern-day protagonist of Smith's experimental short story,
"Horses," who longs for and dreams of horses. At the story's end she
has a vision of an Eohippus, a tiny *dawn horse*, supposed to have
been the ancestor of the horse and extinct for 45 million years. The
protagonist, whose husband runs a body shop – as in cars – runs to
save the dawn horse from the trap that she has set for wild stallions.
But the trap has disappeared (*Cakewalk*, 210).[6] According to
Friedrich, "Indo-Europeanists recognized long ago that Baltic Saule
was close in meaning to the Greek, Italic, and Indic Dawn figure.
They also recognized that the form was cognate with the semantically
related forms for the Vedic sun god and goddess and with a large set
of forms for 'sun' in many other stocks: Latin *sol*, Old Irish *suil*, and
so forth" (Friedrich, 36).

Common features of these Indo-European sun and dawn goddesses and the Near Eastern goddesses of war and sex – such as the
Sumerian Inanna, the Ishtars of older Akkadian, and the many Ishtars
and Ishtar-like figures of the Semitic area, including the Phoenician
Astarte – are the color red and rising from the bath. Before we turn to

compare these characteristics with Almarine's first sight of Red Emmy, we should also consider the Old Irish evidence, for this is most likely the line of mythology Smith was heir to in her mountain materials. Joseph Campbell traces a prehistorical diffusion from Crete, the birthplace of Aphrodite, through Gibraltar to Ireland,[7] and Robert Graves points out that Irish myths "have been, on the whole, less severely edited than the Greek."[8] In fact, Red Emmy's name, with its *r* and double *m*, may echo the Morrigan, the great Irish war goddess who sprang from the same ancient complex as Inanna.

Let us turn now for comparison to the sight that stamps Almarine's life:

The woman whirled around. She stood. Now everything that happened, happened real fast of course, but for Almarine it was like it taken a hundred years. She seemed to turn so slow, and her hair whirled out slow as she turned, like a red rain of water around her head. In his mind he would see her again and again, the way she stood up so slow and how she turned.

"Git outen here," she said.

But she made no move to cover her glory and Almarine looked his fill. She was a woman as big as he was, a woman nearabout six feet tall. Her eyes was as black as night and her nose was long and thin. Her mouth was as red as a cut on her face and the color flamed out in her cheeks. It was a long face. Bony. But Almarine thought she was beautiful. Her hair hung all down her back like one of them waterfall freshets along the path and her breasts were big and white with her nipples springing out on them red as blood.

"My name is Almarine Cantrell," he said, "and I aim to take you home." (*Oral,* 44)

Before we turn to further consideration of the character of Red Emmy, it is necessary to ask why Almarine is not destroyed when he comes upon the goddess bathing. In most Greek myths, when a mortal comes upon a goddess bathing he does not live to tell the story, as when Actaeon similarly stumbles upon Artemis. Challenging, "Tell that you have seen the goddess naked if you can," she splashes water on him, whereupon he turns into a stag and is torn to bits by his own hounds. Yet Almarine sees Red Emmy and lives. Perhaps Almarine is a god. In this case Red Emmy is a sun goddess and he is a water god. Among the Balts existed "a female solar figure and a male aquatic one . . . the heavily erotic fire-in-water theme has many variations and ramifications in Indo-European" (Friedrich, 46).

The sound correspondence between Red Emmy's name and the Morrigan reverberates in light of "You have to get their names right" from *Black Mountain Breakdown* and in light of Friedrich's raising the "general issue that language is a set of relations between a system of sound and a system of meaning, both of which it includes" (Friedrich, 201). He suggests that correspondences of meaning between myths, especially when they are complex and many-sided and borrowing has been ruled out, may be constituted, and thus reconstituted, by sound. The issue is important as novelists like Smith in *Oral History* and Toni Morrison in *Song of Solomon*, two novels whose plots lead back to the cave for recovery of lost meaning, search for lost sacred names obliterated by the patriarchy. Similarly, the African American community, in naming its children, often seems to seek a correspondence of sound with African languages. Reducing the names of god to one seems too reductive for the searching, imaginative human spirit.

Red Emmy is Inanna, the sacred and sexual, potent and alarming female driven out of civilization, just as she is in *Oral History*. Dory is Aphrodite, Pearl is Venus; the whole story of these fallen women traces a mythico-religious history that follows chronological lines. Smith has said that she could not find mythic roles for women until she returned to her mountain material. Not only are mountains loci for the worship of these goddesses, but in Smith's narrative Appalachian Celtic materials still inform fairy tales and song. The Old Irish Morrigan were a trio of sisters – war and sex goddesses associated with the color red and with cattle – who predate the Greek Aphrodite.

Red Emmy's name contains the consonant sounds of Morrigan. Further suggestive evidence that this occupies a niche in Smith's imagination is found in the name Fay – recalling the residual Morrigan, Morgan le Fay – in her next novel and intensified in the reference to the phenomenon of the Fata Morgana in "Intensive Care" – the other place where the goddess emerges from the water in Smith's fiction. Cherry Oxendine's daughter copies out for a school report that the Fata Morgana is "described as a rare and beautiful type of mirage, constantly changing, the result of unstable layers of warm and cold air. The Fata Morgana takes its name from fairy lore and is said to evoke in the viewer a profound sense of longing" (*Eclipse*, 183).

But the sounds *m* and *r,* common to Red Emmy and the Morrigan, are also found in *mother.* (They are also echoed in Ora Mae, which makes her a dark and potent side of this same complex.) In the character of Red Emmy, Smith tries to restore the sexuality of the myth, to redeem red. In the cultural idiom, red became unacceptable and faded to pink as female sexuality was muted and suppressed; concomitantly, the woman in red was vilified–and so she is in Smith's fiction. It is not considered possible to be both genuinely erotic and genuinely kind, to be both sexual and trustworthy. The woman in red was degraded for her very power: her power to move and to create–in short, her sexuality. And it is not just her sexuality that has been degraded, but everyone's, for it is not just female psychology but sexuality itself that our culture has failed to understand and has damaged. The most fundamental thing we have failed to understand is that mother became mother by being sexual; in sacred iconography the Mother Mary obliterates that human truth.[9]

The "heavily erotic fire-in-water theme" helps explain the power of the scene where Red Emmy, color flaming out in her cheeks and indeed all over her, rises from the water, her hair a red rain. But the mention of "a female solar figure and a male aquatic one" forces us to look more closely at Almarine's name. The first element, *Al-,* mimics the beginning of *Allah,* the Muslim name for god, and echoes *El,* the Hebrew name for god (such an identification may be further encouraged in the name of Almarine's son, Eli). In fact, however, *Al-* is Arabic for *the,* which leaves *marine. Almarine* can be rendered either "the sea," a sea god or the primordial deep itself, or "the one from the sea," an Aphrodite figure. It seems indisputable that Almarine can encounter Red Emmy and live because he too is a god. This links him with his own progeny, Dory, whom I will equate with Aphrodite, the goddess who in one version of her genesis arose in the spume of the sea from the castrated parts of her father, Uranus. (Aphrodite is the only sexual female in mythology who is never a virgin and is never raped.) Both the names Almarine and Dory lack *theos* ("god"), although their elements are often linked to *theos.*

From his front door, Almarine looks out on space, like god:

Almarine looks past the creek and the dropping-off holler. Almarine looks out on space. Away across his valley he sees Black Mountain rising jagged to the sky–county seat beyond it, Black Rock where the courthouse is–and if he looks to the left on past it, he sees all the furtherest ranges, line on line. Purple and blue and blue again and smokey until you can't tell the mountains apart from the sky. Lord, it'll make a man think something, seeing that. It'll make a man think deep. (*Oral*, 35)

Black Mountain is named and redeemed in this novel.

Almarine, who communes with the wild animals, screams in the night like a panther until all the panthers scream back. He "trained a crow one time, till it could talk. It could say about fifteen words when his brother Riley kilt it with a rifle, out of spite" (*Oral*, 28). In Old European religion (7500 to 3000 B.C.) the second of the original basic configuration of three main goddesses is the Mistress of Animals or Mistress of Wild Things. There is also a much-rarer Master of Wild Things (Friedrich, 23), an archetype to which Almarine's activities would seem to link him. Training a crow to talk also links him to Red Emmy, who has grown up in a cave with ravens, and the Old Irish "Morrigan[e] and her two sisters usually appear in the form of crows"[10] and are linked to ravens.

Although the connection may be strained, it is worth mentioning that Almarine's name is just the middle consonantal sound (*r* versus the cluster *nd*) off *almandine*, which the *American Heritage Dictionary* defines as "a deep violet-red garnet found in metamorphic rocks and used as a gemstone." (The name Almarine is puzzling at first because it echoes, but is not, *aquamarine*.) The deep violet-red and the gemstone signal our goddess of many names, but what I wish to note here is the metamorphic rock.[11] In *The Last Day the Dogbushes Bloomed* Susan's mother describes Tom Cleveland, her daughter Betty's suitor, as "such a fine, solid, boring citizen. Like a rock, and I quote" (*Last*, 108). But metamorphic rock is capable of transformative change, and Smith has commented about the end of *Black Mountain Breakdown* that she believes in adult change (pers. comm., 1989). A further argument for mention of this gemstone close to the name Almarine is that for the second Almarine, living in the demythologized modern world, gemstones are just steps in AmWay. Furthermore, Jennifer, making her way up to the haunted family cabin, finds and discards as cheap a strand of green glass beads, which were once a present for Dory. In the world of AmWay and sparkling "Foxy Lady" T-shirts, the meaning of sparkling gemstones, treasures from the earth, is lost.

Both Almarine and Red Emmy come from mysterious origins. His father, "as mean as a snake and hard on women and children" (*Oral*, 28), had come to America under mysterious circumstances, perhaps from Ireland, "by ship, he said, and then by wagon, and they was religion mixed up in it someway, but of course you couldn't never prove it by Van Cantrell. He brung that wife of hisn, that Nell, from Ireland with him, or so we thought, although wasn't nobody sure since she was so ashy-pale and she never said a word until Van went off to fight in the war after which she perked up considerable" (*Oral*, 28-29).

Nell sounds suspiciously like a mythic figure, with her dubious origins. Granny says that "the sweetness and goodness you find in most women were not present . . . in old Nell Cantrell" and that "any sweetness in the family, it went straight to Almarine" (*Oral*, 31).

Red Emmy's genesis is even more mysterious. As far as society can see, she lives alone with her father, Isom, up under the Raven Cliffs. To clinch the fact that she is a very ancient figure from prehistory, we are told that she "growed up with ravens, in caves" (*Oral*, 46). Isom's name is unusual, too, perhaps recalling "I am." Apparently he and Granny Younger were once mates: "They was a time once when me and Isom—but Lord, that's another story. Isom had done gone his way, I'd went mine" (*Oral*, 46). About Emmy, Granny says, "But didn't nobody know how he got that gal. Some says he had him a wife and he kilt her, and others says he just drempt Emmy up outen the black air by the Raven Clifts. Others says he stole him a baby from West Virginia" (*Oral*, 46).

Like other children of Zeus, then, Emmy's birth may have been by androgenesis. Since her father dreamed her, one can argue that she was sprung from his head. This links her to two motherless goddesses: Athena, who sprang from the head of her father, Zeus (whose name is associated with stone), and Aphrodite, who sprang from the testicles of her father, Uranus. Furthermore, ravens were war birds in Old Irish mythology, which links Emmy to the warlike Ishtars and Astarte. This is a woman of power and purpose. In one predictable fate of the devolved goddess, Red Emmy is branded a with by the community, even by Granny Younger herself, who in one of her aspects is the voice of conventional community beliefs and taboos. The suppressed goddess is construed as evil, and Granny tells us that "Isom . . . pledged her to the devil" (*Oral*, 46). This society refuses to see her divinity precisely because she is female, powerful, and sexual.

When Almarine says he "aim[s] to take [her] home," the sorrow of the denied goddess is poignant: "When he said that, it was like a shadow crossed her face. She looked sadder for a minute than a body has ever looked. She looked like all the sadness in the world was in her heart. She knowed it couldn't happen, that is why" (*Oral,* 44). The Red One could not, in her divinity, be domesticated.

Without belaboring the argument, let me point out that every signal indicates that the meeting of Almarine and Red Emmy is fated; the landscape is literally strewn with markers of the presence of the goddess Friedrich traces from the earliest sun goddesses through the Greek Aphrodite. (Smith is not working from a schema, and associations are loose.) Almarine is out hunting one day on top of Snowman (mountain peaks are sacred to Aphrodite [Friedrich, 74]) at the beginning of spring (Aphrodite's season [Friedrich, 75]) when all the mountain streams are coming unlocked ("Aphrodite's association with water and her birth from whirling foam may be Near Eastern or go back to Old European" [Friedrich, 80]). A red bird, its coloring signalling its identity as an avatar of Aphrodite (Friedrich, 74-75), leads Almarine off the path with a song so sweet that it makes him cry (Aphrodite induces subjective states [Friedrich, 97-100]). His dog is named Duck, so curious a name for a dog that it calls attention to itself. Aphrodite is strongly linked to water birds and may have come from an Old European water bird goddess (Friedrich, 11); other dawn figures are linked to dogs (Friedrich, 215). Duck's name is also important because of Susan's all-male King Dog. Her naming links the animal to a male divine; his naming links his dog to a female divine.

Duck recognizes the presence of the goddess, turns tail, and runs at the sight of the red bird, his hair standing up along his back. As the red bird hops along leading Almarine, a path opens up in front of Almarine's feet where there has never been a path before. Ushas, the Vedic goddess of dawn, "awakens all creatures to *motion.* She reveals paths and makes them easier to traverse, and she does not miss directions" (Friedrich, 38).

Almarine finds himself on the "wild side" of Snowman, where the great white rocks look as if they had been thrown against the side of the mountain by the gods ("They is no rocks like it anyplace

else on any of these three mountains" [*Oral*, 42]). In a place he has
never been before he spies a flower he has never seen before, "in all
his years running these mountains" (*Oral*, 43). It is a yellow flower,
resembling a rose, growing straight up from the rocky ground on a
leafless green stalk. Aphrodite is "diagnostically floral," especially
roses in bloom (Friedrich, 75); the tawny yellow color is hers
(Friedrich, 78). (Yellow roses grew around the house of her mother
the Queen, according to Susan, narrator of *The Last Day the Dogbushes Bloomed*, and Susan puts on a yellow dress at the novel's
end.) To punctuate the magic nature of the interlude, we learn that
Almarine can never find path, bird, or flower again: "It was like it
was all in my mind. Iffen it was or iffen it wasn't, twerent up to me to
say, but I'll say this – iffen a body searches for so long, he's bound to
find something, that's a fact" (*Oral*, 47).

Almarine does indeed find the source (as does Smith, in this
novel). He finds Red Emmy cooking over an open fire in front of her
daddy's cave. Her father drives him away with a gun, but soon thereafter Isom dies, and Emmy comes to Almarine at night:

> It was right at midnight when she come, Almarine asleep on the down tick be-
> side the fire. Duck stood out in the yard a-howling, but she spoke a word and
> it hushed him. Red Emmy pushed open the door with her foot and walked in
> the front room. She laid her poke in the corner. Then she walked over and
> looked down at Almarine where he laid in heavy sleep, his light hair splayed
> out on the piller.
> Lord! What could have went on in that Emmy's head? She knowed she
> could never be no man's wife. She knowed how her daddy had raised her. She
> knowed too what her own needs was and how to fill them. But just right then,
> for a minute, when Emmy looked down at Almarine sleeping, it was like she
> was the one bewitched. (*Oral*, 48)

As we see here, Aphrodite herself is susceptible to the subjective
states she induces in others: "love is not simple" (Friedrich, 61).

It should be manifestly clear by now that in *Oral History* we can
scratch the soil of Appalachia and find ourselves standing on Mount
Olympus. If Red Emmy did throw her father from the heights it
would not be the first time someone was hurled from that peak, but
here it is the young goddess, not the old gods, who is doing the
hurling; it is a reversal in that the patriarch is at stake. Red Emmy
leaps out of the Oedipus myth of the daughter leading around her

blind father and into the Psyche myth of direct connection (Gilligan 1989, 25-27). But Red Emmy goes back much farther, back to between 30,000 and 12,000 years ago, when "Paleolithic people sought out the dark and silent interior of caves" (Perry et al., 4-5), back to whatever precursors bring us the Sumerian Inanna, "the naked goddess we have known since the beginning of time" (Campbell 1987a, 413), the first deity we know who journeyed into the underworld for three days, to save her brother-lover.

The queen of heaven, the daughter of god, goddess of the morning and evening star, the hierodule or slave-girl dancer of the gods – who, as morning star, is ever-virgin but, as evening star, is "the divine harlot," and whose names in a later age were to be Ishtar, Aphrodite, and Venus – "from the 'great above' set her mind toward the 'great below,' abandoned heaven, abandoned earth, and to the nether world descended" to release her brother and spouse from the land of no return (Campbell 1987a, 412, 418). It is a theme that has been given many turns in the course of the centuries since. One thinks, for example, of Mary Magdalene weeping outside the tomb.[12] The secret of the Cantrells – that they "can't tell" – is not only that they have seen the goddess, but that they have seen the goddess naked.

Pricey Jane

With Pricey Jane we enter the Neolithic revolution that began some 10,000 to 11,000 years ago (Perry et al., 5), the period of agriculture and the domestication of animals. No longer screaming at panthers, Almarine is a settled farmer; gone is the woman, sexual at dawn. Pricey Jane does not run around in the mountains as Red Emmy did; she stays at home, and Almarine brings it all back. But Pricey Jane is also liminal: she is an orphan who arrives with gypsies. Her dark beauty sparks a memory that Ushas has a sister, Night, bright with stars (Friedrich, 37). It is her sister-goddess Ereshkigal, "the dark side of her own self" (Campbell 1987a, 413), the naked black-haired goddess of the underworld of death and darkness, before whom the queen of heaven, Inanna, appears to free her mate, Damuzi-absu (Tammuz, Adonis), the ever-dying, ever-living god. At each of the seven gates her gemstones and gold are removed, till at the seventh gate all her garments are removed, and, naked, Inanna comes before her sister and the seven judges of the netherworld. She is hanged on a stake for three days. The "oldest recorded account of the passage through the gates of metamorphosis, the Sumerian myth of the goddess Inanna's descent to the netherworld," comes from a Sumerian fragment from the period of the tombs of Ur, ca. 2150-2050 B.C.[13] Even as late as "early Greek . . . the Moon is a sister of Dawn" (Friedrich, 33), and Pricey Jane remembers her mother telling her she was always "mooning" (*Oral*, 68). And a sickness has come into the world, a weariness:

> Her mama's face was white and thin and grainy, and she never said a word about love. She just wouldn't answer Pricey Jane. And then she was always so tired. If you asked her about love, her eyes would glaze over like she couldn't remember how it felt or what it meant or even recognize the word spoken right out loud like that, in air. Or she'd act like there was something shameful in it, something Pricey Jane ought not to know. (*Oral*, 68)

In this passage we glean what little information we have about the provenance and meaning of the earrings that come to be construed as the curse on the Cantrells; they are of more mysterious origin than Pricey Jane herself:

> In some of the songs, love was described as a game, with dosey-do and curtsy and funny responses. In others it was like a sickness. Pricey Jane remembered the song about the two sisters and one of them had drowned herself in a millpond, out of love. It was like a sickness unto death. In any case, Pricey Jane's mother had died before she ever gave any answer, if she had any answer to give. Instead, her mother had given her these earrings, pressing them into her hand. But where had they come from anyway, these beautiful earrings, with the roses traced in gold around the loops? Who had them, in what faraway country, and when? (*Oral*, 69)

Carol Gilligan would argue that the meaning of love has been lost with the damage done female psychology. With the change to permanent settlement came the possession of private property – the sacred sexual female is now possessed in the golden rose earrings. Red Emmy is gone, but a physical reminder of her remains. Pricey Jane's first name indicates her status as a valuable possession, and her disposal as property is underscored by the fact that Almarine trades a mule for her. In Smith's fiction, this connects with the reversal Brooke ponders in *Ripley's Believe It or Not*, about the man who traded his wife for a valise.

Historically, Ireland came under British domination when Red Eva McMurrough's father traded her to the Earl of Pembroke, called "Strongbow," in exchange for defense of his kingdom. I am frankly puzzled over the meaning of the second element of Pricey Jane's name. A dictionary etymology has "Jane" coming from the Old French "Jehane," same as Joan, as in Joan of Arc. But why would Pricey Jane be linked to Joan of Arc? Joan of Arc does figure in Smith's fiction: the narrator of "Tongues of Fire" and Crystal of *Black Mountain Breakdown* think of her, especially in relation to hearing voices or a call. Joan of Arc was called to destiny not only *like* a warrior but *as* a warrior. God spoke directly to her, and although she was condemned to death for heresy, she was burned at the stake like so many women of the time accused of being witches.

Yet Pricey Jane carries the markers of Aphrodite. Her golden rose earrings are unequivocal: golden is the most common epithet for Aphrodite and rose the diagnostic flower. According to Friedrich, "Of the queens, only Aphrodite is intrinsically golden. She is the most golden, and 'golden' is her most frequent epithet . . . [Aphrodite is] diagnostically floral, especially roses in bloom" (Friedrich, 78, 75). Furthermore, Pricey Jane's voice reminds Almarine "somehow of a dove" (*Oral*, 59), and "the amorous dove is one of [Aphrodite's] birds" (Friedrich, 96). "She is often paired with the dove, which appears on her head, at her elbows, or in her hand" (Friedrich, 76). The dove is diagnostic not only of Aphrodite but also of Semitic Astarte; dove shrine, dove goddess (Friedrich, 25-27). Lastly, Pricey Jane is a sexually passionate wife, in contrast with attitudes expressed by other characters: "Two dragonflies mate in the shimmering air above the springhouse, blue in the sun. They fly together, a single enormous glittering dragonfly, and Pricey Jane smiles. 'Hit's a woman's duty and her burden,' Rhoda said. Pricey Jane smiles and fills her buckets at the spring" (*Oral*, 71).

Although Hera is the archetypal mother among the queens of heaven, her negative sides "reflect her anger, resentment, and frustration as a wife" (Friedrich, 84), and it is Aphrodite who "stands at various times for the passionate legitimate wife" (Friedrich, 85). Aphrodite thus "patronizes *the loving and passionate wife* in a way that crucially complements Hera (and Demeter) – a point that has been critically neglected. Such a positive image of the physically passionate wife is also neglected in world religions and similar norma-

tive systems" (Friedrich, 85). Aphrodite fills an emotional and religious gap, representing "on the religious level that part of sexual desire and amorous pleasure (*aphrodisia*) without which the union of
man and woman in marriage cannot find fulfillment" (Friedrich, 84).

Pricey Jane also embodies woman's immanent practice valorized
by Smith as noble and constituting art: "Then she sweeps the yard,
too, making graceful circles in the dust, a pattern of swirls all over
the yard, and it looks real pretty, and Pricey Jane wishes Almarine
would get back in time to see it" (*Oral,* 71). Her short section is one
of the most lyrical passages in the book. She "sings a song without
words as she nurses Dory. The steady pull on her nipple is like a
chain somehow, linking her to Dory and more than that to Almarine,
gone off trading. It's like a chain that closes her in and holds her
here, a chain of her own choosing or dreaming" (*Oral,* 70). In this
sense Pricey Jane, like Joan of Arc, chooses her destiny. She chooses
to be a mother, a destiny possible for women. Smith would not valorize only the destiny of a warrior.

Vashti

Anne Goodwyn Jones characterizes Almarine's relationship with
Vashti as such: "Almarine's third relationship has little of love – and
little of death. Vashti's attraction, for Almarine, is her housework;
romance – and its intense sexuality – has disappeared, to be replaced
only by loneliness and isolation."[14] The historical significance of
Vashti, however, is illuminating, and it follows our time line: Vashti
comes after Red Emmy and Pricey Jane in Almarine's life and in our
chronology. Vashti is a historical figure, perhaps a combination of
mythological goddess and historical figure, which is fitting for *Oral
History.*[15] Whereas Red Emmy and Pricey Jane belong to prehistory
("oral"), cave dwellers and agricultural settlers, respectively, Vashti
brings us for the first time over the border from prehistory to history
and to the legacy of the Judeo-Christian ethic. The story of Vashti is
recorded in the book of Esther (1:9-22). The biblical account has
Vashti as the wife of Ahasuerus (Xerxes I), a Persian king of the
Achaemenian Dynasty (486-465 B.C.), son of Darius the Great. On the
seventh day of an all-male banquet, King Ahasuerus sent for Queen
Vashti to display her naked beauty to his drunken guests, for she was
a beautiful woman. When Vashti refused to come, the king banished
her and proclaimed the edict throughout his empire "that every man

be lord in his own house" (verse 22). This deposal of Vashti led to the search for other beautiful maidens, and eventually to the choice of Esther as the new queen.

Thus the biblical account of Vashti is a landmark in the history of the subjugation of women. The story may well encode the rise of the patriarchy, the fall of the goddess, and the ascendancy of the male-imaged monotheistic tradition:

> The historicity of this account is questionable. Xerxes' queen was Amestris and not Vashti (Herodotus VII.61; IX.108-12). The attempt to identify Vashti with Stateira, the wife of Artaxerxes II, does not seem wholly successful. If the origin of Purim is found in Babylonian mythology, it is possible that Vashti represents an Elamite goddess allied with Haman and Zeresh against the Babylonian Marduk and Ishtar. On the other hand, the role of Vashti in the book of Esther may be simply a fictional device for introducing Esther.[16]

That is, the tale of Vashti results in the elimination of the wife of will, the one who will not show off her body when the patriarch bids, and the substitution of the obedient Esther. Smith puts her Vashti in between, using the name of the ancient one who refused the demands of domesticity for the one who was domesticated.

In our story it means the continual dimming of the radiance of Red Emmy. Vashti's daughter, Ora Mae, will be the stone blocking out the bright light of Dory, who rolls the stone away from the tomb for Richard. Vashti's name may also recall Vesta, Roman goddess of the hearth.

Sexual Passion and Spiritual Love

The long trek of women ends with Dory. She is the last character in *Oral History* who is described as timeless, an eternal presence. This daughter of Pricey Jane is the last full embodiment of Red Emmy. We first glimpse the child-woman through the eyes of Richard Burlage, as he stands in the mountain classroom where he has come to teach. She seems to come in on a shaft of sunlight:

> I clapped the erasers together, raising chalk dust which hung dreamily in the shafts of sunlight that came in the windows.
>
> It was then that she came; it was then she appeared, and stood in the door.

> I must say without preamble that she is the most beautiful woman I have
> ever seen, with an ethereal, timeless, otherworldly quality about her. *(Oral,*
> 118)

Smith has achieved transcendence for her beautiful golden women. Dory is ethereal, but, unlike Crystal, her etherealness is not transient and transparent but timeless and otherworldly, complex and sacred: "She was so lovely–a girl from another world" *(Oral,* 119). Finally, Richard describes her as a divinity: "The sun streamed in the schoolhouse door behind her, turning her curls into a flaming gold halo around her head" *(Oral,* 119).

By now we can identify the divinity, and all the markers are there. The golden Dory is the golden Aphrodite of Greece. Her name is *dor,* pure gold. When *theos* is added to it the unusual name Dory ironically becomes the more common name Dorothy, its sacred origins lost in the demystification of time. In Smith's mythico-religious history, Dory's affair with Richard, the Lion-Hearted on his quest, nods both to the historical period of the Crusades – fitting into our time line – and to the iconography of the goddess of love as accompanied by, or even mating with, a lion (cf. Ishtar's lion and horse lovers [Friedrich, 16]). Dory's later marriage to the lame Little Luther mimics the marriage of Aphrodite to the lame smith Hephaestus.[17] Vexed by his ugliness, his mother, Hera, had cast Hephaestus headlong from the heights of Olympus, causing his lameness *(Iliad* 18.395-96). The name in historical time brings us to Martin Luther and the advent of Protestantism, bearing "the odium of being nothing but a *man's religion* which allows no metaphysical representation of woman."[18] Dory's death by train is a conflation of the industrial revolution and the ushering in of the age of technology with a continuing fall in the status of women. That fall is imaged in its starkest form with the machines of men rolling their hard wheels over the neck of the Golden One as they go into the mountains to plunder its coal; the spur line where Dory dies runs off to a coal tipple. Her death is a sacrifice.

Thus our mythico-religious history is completed, and the outlook would seem to be bleak. Smith is not finished, however. We have not plumbed the contents of the Dory story, or its meaning, and the mere evocation of Dory has in it remarkable insight and hope, which will be fulfilled by Ivy Rowe in *Fair and Tender Ladies.* Smith says that in Ivy Rowe she tried to imagine a woman with the "grace and guts" to sustain life's inevitable losses (pers. comm., 1989).

Whereas Crystal's collapse we attribute to the split between spirit and matter, Dory is that healing presence (i.e., Aphrodite) who bridges the opposition between purity and sex (Friedrich, 147). Uniting spiritual love and sexual passion, putting together sex and religion, she heals a sickness that pervades the world – or, certainly, the relationship between the sexes, which in many ways constitutes the world – and promises wholeness and sacred sex. Dory's abandonment by Richard Burlage, who is on a quest for spiritual and sexual healing himself, is not just a tragedy for them; in historical terms it marks an event – abandonment of the Golden One – that renders society tragic. It is the rejection of the golden goddess Aphrodite – and of all she embodies – by polite, literate culture that marks the going out of light from the world. It means permanent suffering for women and loss for everyone else. Through understanding the complex of Dory we come to understand the predicament of the faded and damaged Aphrodites who haunt Smith's fiction – Crystal, Pearl, Fay of *Family Linen*, Lily of the short story "Not Pictured" – but Dory transcends them and offers a way for their transcendence.

In her provocative essay "The Orality of *Oral History*" Anne Goodwyn Jones elucidates how *Oral History* seeks links between sex and religion and art and prophecy:

> Yet it is infrequent in contemporary thought, and certainly in conventional thought, to find a connection between sexuality and religion. Within the academy, religion is departmentalized and intellectualized, and religious experience, popular mystical experience in particular, is ignored. Within institutionalized religion, the relationship between sexuality and religion is often seen as inverse; the more one follows Jesus, the less one follows the call of the body. There are numerous theological and psychological implications to these positions; my point here is simply that *Oral History* finds an intersection of sexual and religious experience in some interesting and important ways. In the plotting, we are led to make a link between sex and religion. (Jones 1986, 18)

Part of the whole drift of the plotting of *Oral History* involves the entanglement of pagan with Judeo-Christian elements: in addition to the abuse suffered by Red Emmy, Maggie has a happy marriage with a preacher, although she must give up the earrings, and Jennifer marries Bernie Ripman, apparently a Jew from Miami. Of course, when Van and Old Nell came from Ireland "they was religion mixed up in it someway." Subsumed by Judeo-Christian iconography, our knowledge of the goddess is lost.

Friedrich argues that we no longer recognize the goddess of sacred sex because her image has been suppressed. He postulates that she goes all the way back to a suppressed mother/lover archetype and bridges such traditional oppositions as sex and purity. One reason, Friedrich argues, that she has been suppressed is the same reason that she was mocked by the other gods: because of her potency. (That this suppression is still vehemently practiced was made clear when, in the summer of 1991, the same supermarkets–the stomping ground of mothers, after all–that refused to display the magazine *Vanity Fair* because of its dazzling cover photograph [by Annie Leibovitz] of the naked and pregnant actress Demi Moore had no problem displaying magazines like the *National Enquirer* whose covers featured photographs of singer/actress Dolly Parton as a battered woman. No coincidence could make more clear what is, and what is not, acceptable in mainstream American culture at the end of the twentieth century. The sexual mother is not acceptable to the supermarket's magazine stockers; the woman beaten to a pulp is. Hence mothers and children may gaze at length at the battered woman but may not see the beautiful representation of what woman is and how women become mothers.) Historically, the concrete power of the institutionalized church specifically sought the erasure of this sexual-sacred female in the burning of Sappho's poems on Aphrodite and female love:

> Between the first and fifteenth centuries of our era, notably as a consequence of Christianity, 95 percent of her poems were destroyed, most of the estimated 9,000 lines. . . . Some of this rapine occurred during outbursts of Greek Orthodox fanaticism. Some . . . by French and German Crusaders. . . . On several occasions her poems were publicly burned by the order of popes and bishops or by mobs of zealots. This compulsion to burn Sappho indicates that her vision threatened the Christian foundations of patriarchy, hypocrisy, and puritanism. (Friedrich, 126)

The damage done Aphrodite by the institutional church is reinvented by Smith in a section, suppressed by her publisher, written to

explain Red Emmy's difference as a result of her having been sexually
and physically abused by a preacher and his wife who adopted her.
Here in Smith's imagination is a recapitulation of damage done to the
sacred sexual female by patriarchal religion and the women who
collude with it. Her editor recommended that she suppress the section to leave a mystery at the heart of the text. The energy of what is
not expressed unwinds from its central place in Western culture: the
damage done to the sacred by the dominant religion and its defend-
ers in the name of the sacred. It is interesting to speculate if the editor intuited that too specific a rendering of the root cause of the
damage would turn readers away, whereas suppression of the story
would probably elicit empathy among readers who see in Red
Emmy's situation the damage done their own sexual and sensual
selves.

The way patriarchy, hypocrisy, and puritanism encode themselves on individual bodies is shown in the hog-killing ritual of *Oral
History*. As Susan Griffin points out in *Pornography and Silence:
Culture's Revenge against Nature*, the pornographer is the loyal son
of the doctrinal mind. The hog killing, presented as a male initiation
rite that does harm to the sensitive young Jink Cantrell, is marked by
lewdness, with sexist and racist attitudes and language. Not only is
hog flesh being killed and gutted, but flesh itself is being demeaned
by the adult men. In the lewd story Parrott Blankenship tells during
this ritual the nature of the primal cave itself is made blatantly obvious.[19] Parrott's narrative is about "witchery" (*Oral*, 201), of how he
was bewitched by a widow who first rode her own roan horse to
death and then began riding him at night, as the mountain people
claim Red Emmy rides Almarine. Again, the fear of the sexual appetite
of the older, experienced woman surfaces. In Parrott's story, while
he is being ridden by the witch he realizes that she and two omi-
nous-looking male accomplices are piling up stolen treasure in a
cave up a steep rocky mountainside nearly hidden by a "brushy
thicket" (*Oral*, 204). Parrott determines to get the treasure for himself and realizes he has to mark the cave entrance when the men pull
the brush aside and he can see the opening. So, in his horse form, he
drops a "big old pile of shit" (*Oral*, 204). Then, when he escapes the
widow, he trots back over to the cave entrance and "pushed through
with my nose until I had got my head inside that cave" (*Oral*, 204). It
was hot in the cave, which surprised him, and "it had a funny smell

to it, and it was black as the blackest night you have ever seen or ever imagined in all your life" (*Oral,* 204). After hearing a voice calling his name and telling him he will be sorry for what he has done, Parrott "woke up, boys, and I was in the widder's bed with my face in her crack, and I had done benastied myself!" (*Oral,* 205).

It takes Jink "a minute to get it" (*Oral,* 205), the kind of confusion such an initiation ritual is meant to engender, so that when the initiate does "get it," his pride in doing so will bond him to the prurient attitudes of the group. The cave, then, is the original dark hole from which we all emerge into the world and to which men return to deposit their treasures. It is also apparently the dark hole that these men fear, and thus with false bravado defile. Parrott's identity as a "parrot" who repeats cultural biases is revealed in this scenario.

We recall that Red Emmy's cave, where she was cooking, was being guarded by her father with his gun, who drove off Almarine when he came with his gun. But Emmy, who wished to be entered, reputedly threw her father off the rocky cliffs to make entrance possible. It is interesting that the cave is variously viewed as a mystery, a place to discover identity, or a place that is tainted by ownership (Red Emmy's father's guarding it, the stolen treasure of Parrott's story). The same paradox obtains in Toni Morrison's *Song of Solomon,* where Milkman goes to the cave in search of treasure but instead discovers his own identity and abilities.

Another compelling reason for Aphrodite's erasure is the resistance of that cultural framework which came to be known as "the rational mind" to transgress the boundaries it has erected.[20] Central to it is the split between the maternal and sensual, the virgin/whore complex at its most classic: "We seem to be left with a universal and unsolvable conflict between the social forces that unify the roles [of parent and lover] and those that keep them discrete. I assume that these age-old questions are as packed with interest as they ever were" (Friedrich, 8).[21] And now we understand why we laugh so hard at Pearl when she runs away with her student, Donny Osborne, and tells him in Howard Johnson's, "Donny, you know you really ought to order some vegetables. You know you're a growing boy" (*Oral,* 273). Smith is transgressing the boundaries.

She transgresses boundaries with humor, bringing together Adonis and Donnie Osmond in the name of the boy Pearl, who can now be identified as Venus, seduces. The Venus and Adonis myth is here flavored with incest (linking Venus back to Inanna), as Donny is Pearl's high school student and shoots Pearl's brother Billy, rumored to be her lover by then, as he sits rocking. Thus the haunted rocker that rocks at twilight speaks, or at least creaks, of incest. Incest was permitted to the gods and the goddesses, as well as to Egyptian rulers.

But Venus is not Inanna any more than Pearl is Red Emmy. A devolution has occurred. That devolution is imaged in *Oral History* with a long falling off from Red Emmy and Almarine on the mountainside all the way down to Pearl and Donny Osborne in Howard Johnson's. The dolls Pearl's daughter Jennifer collects – female images neither sacred nor sexual – are a far cry from the potent Venus of prehistory. The second Almarine's smashing kiss makes Jennifer see stars. This hints that he may share the astral nature of the Aphrodite/Venus complex. The kiss also smacks of incest – in Jennifer's mind at least, although in truth there is no blood relation between them. But the kiss seems invasive rather than erotic. Monaghan, in *The Book of Goddesses and Heroines*, traces the devolution back to the Greeks:

> The energy that Aphrodite represented, however humanly true, was almost incompatible with Greek culture. The Great Goddess of impersonal, indiscriminate lust meshed poorly with the emerging Greek intellectualism. Thus the tale of the goddess's love for the ever-dying god ceased to be central to her legend and became that of just another casual attraction to a pretty face. The rather smutty little tale is a far cry from those masterpieces of theological understanding, the stories of Ishtar, Inanna, and Cybele, with their symbolic description of the hopeless love of the earth herself for the life she continually produces and consumes. (Monaghan, 24)

Liminality

Aphrodite, Inanna, Ishtar, Astarte, Venus, the Morrigan – this goddess with many names stands for the reconciliation of opposites. Like floods, like passion, she brings together things that have been held apart. The insight of Victor Turner's work on liminality is important here. Expanding on Arnold Van Gennep's notions, Turner uncovers the ways in which changes and turnovers happen in liminal (in-between) states, in those interstices where structures are released and new kinds of structures can be built.[22] Friedrich describes the

liminal, from the Latin word for "threshold," as "dynamic or proces-
sual in that it involves crossing over (out of or in to) relatively stable
or fixed structures or 'grids' " (Friedrich, 132). Or it may be interstitial, "operating 'betwixt and between' the margins of these recognized and accepted categories, rules, groups, and structures"
(Friedrich, 132).

One of the great works or jobs of myth, in any case, is to bridge
or simply to assert contradictory categories – to split, rearrange, and
reclassify them – or, in other words, to make it possible for culture to
be dynamic. The emotional mediation provided by liminal phenomena is one of the essential mechanisms by which man "constructs
powerful, pervasive, and perduring moods and motivations . . . by
clothing conceptions with such . . . credibility as to make [them]
uniquely realistic" (Friedrich, 134). But this interstitial or marginal
action also unquestionably releases enormous social and psychological energies that may threaten structures or even destroy them.
On the other hand, these released energies may motivate the building of structures, art, and science. The historic role of Aphrodite is
artistic, notably poetic; inspiration is consonant with this.

Friedrich sums up Aphrodite's liminality as eightfold: "It appears
in association with (a) sexual intercourse without pollution, (b) sexual relations between a goddess and a mortal, (c) the naked goddess,
(d) the active female, (e) the patroness of courtesans, (f) passionate
sexual relations within marriage, (g) nature and culture, and (h) the
'blessings' versus the 'curse' of Aphrodite" (Friedrich, 134).

In many ways, then, the liminality of Aphrodite dwells in our
text, occupying her place of old in "sanctuaries on mountain peaks,
shrouded in mist, the liminal country of shepherds and nymphs and
the abodes of gods in the early Greek and Phoenician world view"
(Friedrich, 146). Most significantly, she brings together sexual passion and spiritual passion:

> If the theory of liminality is ignored, the Aphrodite of the ancient Greeks can-
> not be understood theoretically. Her religious meaning springs not just from
> the fact that she symbolizes fertility and procreation, the joys and curses of
> love, but from her extreme liminality within a system of culturally specific reli-
> gious categories. To adapt Turner: she bridges physical reality and metaphysi-
> cal belief. (Friedrich, 134)

In *Oral History* Smith manages a crossing over between antitheses that she had tried, but not negotiated, in earlier work. The dialectic that troubles, even paralyzes, characters in earlier novels provides the creative tension to sustain this ambitious work. In this novel Smith is able practically and artistically to find the interstitial zone between Richmond and the mountains, and the border struggle explodes to find those borders between present and past, written and oral, culture and nature, socioeconomic group and human community, rationalism and intuition, mind and body, head and heart, duty and beauty, form and essence, controlling and letting go, matter and spirit. I submit that she succeeds in bridging these heretofore mutually destructive opposites because, in her recovery of mythic contents, Smith recovers the lost psychological complex – interstitial, liminal, transgressive – we call Aphrodite.

I am not saying that Smith deliberately set out to do any of these things. In fact, I believe that she did not. It is a revelation and reveals her life's work. She works both consciously and unconsciously and is sufficiently complex, as are the processes of imagination, history, and writing, so that the merger of opposites occurs. Smith wrote her way through patriarchy to get to a sacred-sexual imaging of the female. When she filled in that imaging, those women shared much in common with the goddesses humanity had long ago created. Whatever Smith's rememberings, conscious or subconscious, of those ancient stories (tales of mythic women get told often in the mountains, and we know that she studied mythic materials at Hollins under Richard Allen), Smith gave them voice – and life – in the present.

In *Oral History* Smith has created an altered world that unleashes the female imaging from its bonds, psychic and societal, and out of those fertile waters arise the red and the golden goddesses. I am convinced that she is not writing out of a schema; that would be manipulation rather than creation. The work would not ring true, and it does ring true. It is begotten, not made, of one being with the writer. Smith says that she writes for self-repair and that the need to write was so urgent it nearly consumed her. After finding nothing but wasteland, she finally managed to reconstruct spontaneously in the present those ancient materials that arise from a full mind. And she did it because it was psychologically necessary, as we see from the complete collapse of her heroine at the end of her previous novel. In claiming this rich heritage, Smith found a psychological complex strong enough to counter the collapse of the female psyche in Crystal Spangler.

When we consider Brooke flinging herself down in the snow and making an angel before begging Houston for sex, Susan praying fervently to the evening star, the sexually direct Dory with her flaming gold halo, it is tempting to whisper that Aphrodite herself is the incarnation of that intersection of sex and religion which, as Anne Goodwyn Jones points out, *Oral History* seeks (Jones 1986, 18). In the novel's preoccupation with the prophecies of women (and the first oracles were all women, Apollo notwithstanding) all the way from Granny Younger and Rose Hibbitts to Ora Mae's taking a Rolaids to ward off the warning in her breast, and its seeking an intersection between art and prophecy, it is tempting to whisper that the artist, Smith, is Aphrodite's prophet.[23]

Chapter Six

Wounds Also Heal: *Family Linen*

Smith's sixth novel turns from the high passion of *Oral History* back to more domestic matters, as the title indicates. A rich repository of hard-won wisdom, *Family Linen* recombines many of Smith's themes and stances, softened and deepened by maturity and experience. Smith continues to explore the bridge between generations that gave *Oral History* its fullness, that necessary link to "formal worldmaking and humanness."[1] The writer of *Family Linen* suggests that the most enduring structure, the family, need not be a rigid one. The novel works this theme out narratively, weaving its voices; architecturally, in its emphasis on different kinds of houses; and thematically, with its families breaking up and recombining in a way to make room for everyone.

This novel of reconciliation is again set in southwest Virginia and turns on a mystery in a family. Using a real-life story for a springboard, Smith plumbed her sense that the family is a mysterious entity. The family in *Family Linen* is as damaged as the families in Smith's previous novels – certainly many of its women are damaged in the same ways as Smith's earlier female characters – but for the first time Smith moves beyond the damage to discover that wounds also heal. She has remarked that, as the book jacket cleverly illustrates with its picture of the perfect place setting on the front soiled by cake crumbs on the back, the novel should have been called *Dirty Wash* (pers. comm., 1989). Three generations of the Hess family, which is on its way to healing from terrible disruptions, have plenty of dirty linen. This washing must be done.

Family Linen does its wash in 17 sections comprised of "the downstage narrative voice" ("Voice," 100) – modulated to express different attitudes toward different characters – mixed with dialogue, interior monologues, and a journal of heightened Victorian rhetoric similar to the journals in *Black Mountain Breakdown* and *Oral His-*

tory. Smith seems compelled to explore the Victorian sensibility through its language, especially the lives of women in their families.

The Mythic Past

Family Linen returns to the present to find means of recovery from a damaging past. The epigraph, from *The Go-between* by L. P. Hartley, reads, "The past is a different country; they do things differently there."[2] The way the novel develops suggests that the epigraph may mean that redemption is possible in time. People need not be bound by the past; they can go beyond the way things were done in that "different country." The go-between (the liminal figure) is the writer, who sees past and present and can imagine the future, and who has access to the characters' inner and outer lives.

The epigraph further links this sixth novel to the new knowledge gained in Smith's fifth, as the go-between signals the presence of Aphrodite, going between – even transgressing boundaries – to perform her essential, life-giving function. Not only does Hartley's title nod to the concerns of *Oral History*, but it recapitulates them in that the pivotal scene of *The Go-between* tugs at the same knot as the central scene of *Oral History* – the stamp set on a man's life by the sight of the goddess naked. In Hartley's novel, a boy comes upon the primal scene in a barn where two lovers, who have been using the boy as a go-between, keep their assignation. The boy, who has fallen in love with the woman himself, stumbles on the lovers as they rock as one. He sees the goddess naked, and the sight ruins his life.

Mythic contents continue to inform the fiction, beginning with naming. Sybill certainly plays the function of oracle in her revelation of the family secret. Fay – namesake of Morgan le Fay, a mysterious figure of Arthurian legend usually represented as a sorceress or siren – shows all the damage done to that once-healing, aggressive and active, sacred and sexual female power.[3] And it is interesting to speculate on Nettie as a namesake of Neti, Sumerian mythological gatekeeper of the underworld ruled by Inanna's sister and enemy, Ereshkigal.[4] As for Myrtle, the *Oxford English Dictionary* says that the myrtle was held sacred to Venus and was used as an emblem of love. Myrtle's affair with an exterminator thus seems contradictory, as we consider Venus-Aphrodite's life-giving function, and it well may be. Because Myrtle's every effort is to maintain a certain image, she does not live out of her own nature. On the other hand, the war and sex goddesses who are the precursors of Venus-Aphrodite deal death as well as inspire passion. Smith's impulse brings together the good mother and the bad mother.

Don Dotson's affinity for Fay's daughter, Candy, the novel's Aphrodite, identifies him as another liminal figure, Hermes.[5] Moreover, his role as doctor links him to Nettie/Neti, as Hermes carried shades into and out of the underworld. (The caduceus of Hermes is the symbol of the medical profession.) Don, as we see by his name, is another Adonis, like Donny Osborne. He may also be seen as either an Eros or an Aeneas (or even conflicted between these two sons of Aphrodite/Venus). His last name – Dotson, or "son of Dot," a nickname for Dorothy – suggests his identity as the son of Dory, or Aphrodite (Eros?). Looking back to *Oral History*, he may be the son of Donny and Pearl (Aeneas?). But more happily, he looks forward to Honey Breeding, the Aphrodite male in *Fair and Tender Ladies*. Smith's healing imagination works toward a better fate for these characters.

Smith said she wanted to name the book *Lives of the Stars*, which would point to the centrality of Fay's fevered reading of the *National Enquirer* (with lives of Hollywood stars), the last repository of mystery in a demythologized age, as well as to the astral dimension of Aphrodite figures, lingering in the name of the evening star. (Both Greek Aphrodite and Roman Venus were astral [Friedrich, 80].) But her publisher did not like the title. She says she "got mad and refused to think of another title, so the editorial assistant's boyfriend's mother's suggestion of *Family Linen* stuck" (pers. comm., 1991).

Many of Smith's characters, with their familiar obsessions, emerge in *Family Linen*, but they are more exquisitely and deeply rendered. By drawing upon the mythic past in *Oral History*, Smith was able to construct her female in a different way and to see her as both sacred and sexual. She was also able more clearly to see society's role in the female's destruction, as shown in the definitive sacrifice of Dory. These insights then allow her to take her characters farther, more deeply into their pain, and to begin to find some ways of healing. This applies to both males and females. As society's rigid boundaries are transgressed, males and females can take characteristics society had ascribed to one or the other; both can become more whole. Her own growth is measured in her deeper compassion for her characters and their greater complexity. Her shifting allegiance to the givers in the course of her fiction-writing career, culminating in *Family Linen* in the characters of Don and Candy, takes the edge off her satire and alleviates the crippling vision of her earlier novels: the cure is generosity of spirit. The way to avoid being crippled by seeing how things are – the gift that debilitates Georgia Rose and that Ora Mae refuses, causing shrinking of her own soul – is accepting what one sees.

Release

As in *Oral History,* Smith hits upon the organizational device of a mystery in a family's past for *Family Linen.* The novel's impetus was a story of madness and murder in a family, called "the outhouse murder" by newspapers. In the newspaper account a North Carolina woman who began suffering from debilitating migraine headaches in middle age consulted a hypnotist. Under hypnosis she recovered a repressed memory from her childhood. She remembered seeing her mother kill her father, hack him up with an ax, and dump his body into the outhouse. Her story was apparently verified when police found a man's remains at the spot where the family outhouse had stood. As a result, the North Carolina woman's headaches disappeared. Recovering her memory of the past released its hold on her and relieved her unconscious suffering.

This real-life murder and the 1969 murder of Susan Nason described in Chapter 2 form a startlingly symmetrical pair. In light of Smith's fictive concerns, it would seem that the wounding is a failure to understand sexuality. Jewell Rife is, after all, an Aphrodite male, whose first name (probably also a pun on the "family jewels") suggests his worth. His last name is the same as the cynical preacher of *Oral History,* Aldous Rife, whose bitterness comes from the rape of his sexuality by the mores of conventional religion. Jewell, who seems reprehensible in *Family Linen,* will be redeemed by the Aphrodite male who shares so many of his traits, Honey Breeding. And Jewell's mating with Fay, after all, produces Candy.

Sybill is based on the North Carolina woman with the migraines, although the novel's other characters too struggle for the same release from unconscious suffering. Both *Family Linen* and *Oral History* vacillate between release and confinement. In these novels Smith is finally able to abandon the confinement of artificial and distorting patterns – the boxes of *The Last Day the Dogbushes Bloomed* into which Susan wished to fragment her mind; the graduation figure, kaleidoscope, paperweight, and personality split through which Brooke struggled for control in *Something in the Wind;* that most inhuman and abstract of all, the isosceles triangle of *Fancy Strut;* and perhaps even the crystal of *Black Mountain Breakdown.* In *Oral History* the diagrammed sentences of *Black Mountain Breakdown* break down, both in Granny Younger's lyrical mountain dialect and in Richard's prose when it breaks free through the healing release of emotion. Smith seems to feel more free to let nature run its course. The flood that destroyed Susan's wading-house animals in *The Last Day the Dogbushes Bloomed* emerges as redemptive in *Oral History,* when it brings together Richard and Dory, and is salvific in the Hess family of *Family Linen.* Chaos and force can bring about release and reintegration as well as destruction. The headache of *Family Linen* is a curse that ultimately becomes a blessing, because it is freeing.

Smith began *Family Linen* by imagining what kind of woman would have that kind of headache and came up with Sybill Hess, one of her repressed and judgmental women and one of the many Smith characters whose Greek name spells trouble. Her name suggests both the Greek oracle and the schizophrenic woman with multiple personalities whose story was published in a book similarly named. Through Sybill, the oracle of the murder, the source of the repression and judgment is made clear: the source is pain. Because the same was true of Ora Mae in *Oral History,* it seems possible that pain may be the source of the harshness exhibited by all such women in Smith's fiction.

Smith substituted a well for the outhouse. She took the writer's option to create a more life-affirming symbol. In a sense, the washing motif in *Family Linen* is made blatantly obvious by the construction of a pool on the well site. It is this pool into which the whole family jumps during a wedding reception at the novel's conclusion – in a lemminglike show of family solidarity.

A murder committed more than 40 years earlier is revealed when Sybill consults a hypnotist for relief from her chronic headaches. Except for Sybill's memory, we have no direct view of the murder. In fact, one of the novel's most important characters, the family matriarch, Elizabeth Bird, has died at the beginning of the novel. We are given her girlhood journal, "Days of Light and Darkness–Memoirs," when it is found after her death. The rest of her story comes in a reminiscence by her sister Nettie. Miss Elizabeth grows up an idealistic girl at the turn of the century in Booker Creek, Virginia, "in the mountains, close to the North Carolina line."[6] Her father is a huge mountain man whose lumber business is ruined by bad management. Her mother is a gentlewoman from the "Eastern shore of Virginia" (*Linen*, 168). When her mother dies, 12-year-old Elizabeth is left to care for her sisters, Nettie, seven, and Fay, five. Fay has suffered brain damage during a difficult birth. Nettie grows up becoming more practical, and Elizabeth withdraws into an imagined refinement. When Jewell Rife, a drifter with charming manners, comes to the Bird home to do odd jobs, Elizabeth is captivated. They marry, and Elizabeth gives birth to a daughter, Sybill, and a son, Arthur. Jewell's character is revealed as he proceeds to dissipate the family fortune in loose living. According to Nettie's recollections late in the novel, she goes to the family home one day to confront Elizabeth with rumors that have alarmed her and witnesses a terrible scene through a window. Jewell is sitting at the table while the simple-minded Fay washes dishes at the kitchen sink. Jewell suddenly bangs his hand on the table and calls out "Fay!":

> While I watched her, Fay backed up to the sink and hiked up her skirt and hoisted herself up there, on the edge of the counter, spraddling her legs. She didn't have on any drawers. Then Jewell was at her, his trousers down around his feet, didn't even bother to take them off, fucking her. That's all. He never kissed her, or nothing. He was just fucking her. And the worst part about it was Fay's face, which I could still see, I could see her face all the time, over Jewell's back, above his white shirt. Her face had changed from that waiting, knowing look into something terrible where wanting and hating went back and forth. (*Linen*, 234)

According to Nettie's recollection of this event, she seems to see Fay's mind, never strong, become deranged:

Soon enough, Jewell was done. He flopped his head down over her shoulder, and let his hands drop too, he was breathing hard. Fay stopped making the singing sounds. She was staring straight out to the cold-pantry where I was watching. Now I know she couldn't see me, out there in the dark. I don't think she could have seen me at all. But a look came into her eyes for just a minute, it was the strangest thing, like she *could* see me, and like she was a reasonable person after all, a girl with good sense. This look said, *I know what I'm up to. I know.* And it was all pain. This was pain so pure it was like a real thing twisting and yelling in the air between her and me. Then while I still watched, that was gone and gone entirely, nobody home. Nothing there except Fay's sweet blank expression the way it was before he said "Fay!" the way it always was. (*Linen,* 234)

Shortly thereafter Jewell Rife disappears. According to Sybill's memory under hypnosis, she saw a woman – it is apparently never made clear in the novel whether it is her mother or Fay – kill Jewell Rife with an ax and throw his body into the well. Nettie and Elizabeth take the pregnant Fay away until the child, a daughter named Candy, is born. When they return to Booker Creek, Elizabeth raises Candy as her own child. Nettie speculates on Elizabeth's character as Elizabeth gains the sympathy of the townspeople, who believe that Jewell Rife got her pregnant for a third time and then abandoned her:

Poor, poor Elizabeth! I have to admit I wondered, later, whether Elizabeth was that calculating, to have figured on the impression she wanted to make, returning. I don't think so. Elizabeth was a proud woman with a will like a piece of iron pipe, and the ability to see and hear exactly what she chose to, but she was not conniving. A conniving woman would have seen through Jewell in the first place, remember, or would have figured out how to keep him, and keep him in line. (*Linen,* 251)

Nettie's view of her sister may be a bit generous. From the indications we have of Miss Elizabeth's character, she may be perfectly capable of such conniving.

Verner Hess, a small redheaded man who runs the local five-and-dime, marries Elizabeth, whom he has always loved. They have two daughters, Myrtle and Lacy. He becomes the stable figure in the children's lives. As they grow up, Sybill becomes a compulsive perfectionist, Myrtle takes on her mother's obsession with appearances, and Lacy inherits her mother's love of language, the reason Elizabeth gives in her journal for converting from the Methodist to the Episco-pal church.

Community

Although *Family Linen* returns to satire, it is not just satiric: it shows care, compassion, and respect for people and the ways they struggle with their lives; it allows for community. Here Smith is certain that the lives of women are important, that what they do is important. This tenderness first appeared and was developed in the short sto-ries; in *Oral History* it became possible in an imagined past, but not in the present. In *Family Linen*, however, it is imaginable in the pre-sent. The characters are capable of growth and even forgiveness. De-spite the difficulties inherent in understanding other human beings, the characters in *Family Linen* struggle to help. Despite their va-garies and lapses, or the mutilated ways in which they cope with family relationships, they are capable of a humanity. *Family Linen* is a more forgiving vision of humanity – still hilarious, given Smith's comic flair, but there is something different here.

Smith says she is interested in the mystery of families. Perhaps the way families work is by forcing us to face the truth about other human beings and ourselves. One part of the mystery, as this novel makes clear, is the secret inner life of individuals within a family. The opening uses the device of stories like "Cakewalk" and "The French Revolution: A Love Story," where a rigid worldview is smashed by the messiness of life. We see this messiness as in earlier novels in the same struggles to loosen the structure of family and society so that they do not block knowledge of the world or contact with life.

Family Linen explores this theme through a focus on houses, what they look like and what they contain. Sean, the 14-year-old son of Don and Myrtle, thinks as he rides his bike through their subdivi-sion, "I know who lives in most of these houses. Who the hell ever knows what goes on inside?" (*Linen*, 142). The tension between the internal reality and external façade is a theme we have seen in the preoccupation with houses and structures in *Black Mountain Breakdown* and *Oral History*. But *Family Linen* demonstrates the magnitude of reconciliation achieved in the return to the ancestral home: here the attempt to loosen the structure to accommodate everyone – especially with the swimming pool – is far more successful. One of the most comic articulations of this theme is Nettie's house, with its ramshackle additions to accommodate all the misfits she takes in. As a makeshift architect, Nettie may be dreadful; as a reflection of the way humans live, however, she comes far closer than Sybill and Myrtle's perfect *Southern Living* façades.

Miss Elizabeth does not see houses, or anything, clearly. Her memoir opens, "I approach the Past as a young maiden, bearing a candle, might approach a deserted mansion deep within the Enchanted woods" (*Linen,* 164). The wind blows Miss Elizabeth's candle out at the end of her overwrought recollections of girlhood. She remains willfully blind, and her inability to face reality leaves a terrible legacy. Here Smith illustrates the problem of the feverish imagination that cannot be brought into the open light of day. Yet even Miss Elizabeth is not entirely unredeemed in this novel. She is strong; she holds the family together through the worst of traumas. She raises Candy, the bastard child of her husband and her brain-damaged sister. She ensures the family's continuity and maintains the ancestral home, which in the end is healing. Yet, paradoxically, her way of establishing continuity – by refusing to admit what has happened – leaves the burden of confronting and dealing with reality to those who follow.

The family of Miss Elizabeth are either fleeing from reality or struggling to contact it. The most damaged characters in *Family Linen* flee from the world in various ways – Sybill is frigid, Myrtle is rigid, and Fay is completely insane – and one, Clinus, has agoraphobia, a fear of open spaces that in him, as in all of these characters, is manifested by an inability to leave home. Yet even Clinus tries to communicate with the world by messages on the billboard outside his junk shop. Sybill and Myrtle share with characters from Smith's earlier fiction a preoccupation with appearance and a refusal to enter human suffering. Only Candy, Smith's heroine, is free. And she is not Miss Elizabeth's daughter, but Fay's – the child born of male violence and female submission, but going beyond.

The Characters

The by-now familiar constellation of female characters includes sisters, and this novel has two sets of them. In the first generation we have Miss Elizabeth, the familiar Smith female character who never really marries, sustaining a pristine, old-maidish illusion of a genteel life. Her sister Nettie, who eventually finds a happy marriage – although it requires enduring two unhappy ones – and raises orphaned boys after her only child, a daughter, dies, is one of Smith's down-to-earth survivors. Fay and Nettie are paired aunts of the boys, with one playing what society has labeled a feminine role and the other what society has labeled a masculine role, like the aunts in *Black Mountain Breakdown*.

Fay's name is linked to Morgan le Fay, who was originally the Morrigan, the great Irish war goddess who sprang from the same ancient complex as Inanna, the first deity, the naked goddess we have known since the beginning of time. The case for identification of "Fay" with "Morgan le Fay" is much strengthened by the "Fata Morgana" – a "rare and beautiful type of mirage, constantly changing, the result of unstable layers of warm and cold air" that "takes its name from fairy lore and is said to evoke in the viewer a profound sense of longing" (*Eclipse*, 183) – in Smith's short story "Intensive Care."[7] When Fay dies in an overheated car, believing a man is coming to take her on a trip, ironies abound. Morgan le Fay was on the barge that took Arthur to Avalon for the healing of his wounds. Furthermore, Avalon was the island home[8] of the healing-destroying Morrigan. (As if matters were not complicated enough – no one ever said Lee Smith did not have a good ear – the name Fay is of dubious etymology, coming from either *fai*, meaning "faith," or *faie*, meaning "fairy." This gives the name, like that of Vashti, a double twist, calling into question all lore – maybe biblical, maybe goddess.) Fay continues Smith's exploration of female victims; she is an extension of Crystal, but here she is physically damaged into passivity.

And then we have a second-generation constellation of sisters: Sybill is rigid, controlling, and repressed; Myrtle, who could be an older Monica Neighbors, keeps her "perfect" marriage going by shoring herself up with clichés but is so detached from herself as to take a virtually anonymous lover; Candy, a beautician "by choice" (*Linen*, 37), is warm and life-affirming, the lifelong love of Myrtle's husband, the dermatologist Don Dotson, whose license plate reads "SKIN"; and Lacy, inheritor of the struggle with language and authenticity of Susan and Brooke, is understandably bogged down by her dissertation in English at the University of North Carolina at Chapel Hill and by her fight to reconstruct her life after abandonment by her husband.

In contrast to the constellation of sisters is a brother, a minor character named Arthur. Although not cynical like the brothers in earlier novels, he is a failure. His name, Arthur, suggests that he is a *rex inutilis* ("useless king"). His identity is further linked to the historic Arthur by his Aunt Fay's link to Morgan le Fay. If Fay is a faded goddess then certainly her nephew Arthur is a faded knight, and so we understand better his plight. (The name Arthur probably means "bear" and may go back to a bear goddess, "a goddess of plenty, a mother goddess of all life and food" [Markale, 92].) Grieving for his estranged wife and two daughters, he is consumed with a comic despair and rage. A failed rock-and-roll singer turned alcoholic housesitter, Arthur is not unlikable, and whatever damage he does is self-inflicted. Ironically, at the end of *Family Linen* he happily couples with a nurse.

But as we see how Smith makes use of her stock characters, we shall see, in closer examination of each major character, how she allows for a more complex and positive reading. What is different here is that all the women's quests are ennobled in a way as never before. They are complex, rich, painful, and yet more often redemptive. They are all, or almost all, made mythic, and in different ways: all are bits of Artemis, Hera, and Aphrodite, stuck in Virginia trying to construct viable lives in unbearable situations.

Sybill

The book opens with Sybill, who "approves of order with all her heart" (*Linen,* 17) and has blocked passion – and finally human contact and feeling – from her life. The pathology of such characters in the Smith pantheon is clearly elucidated in this woman, whose name suggests the splitting off of the self. This splitting occurred because of the horrible reality she witnessed; clinging to order was a way to survive, but with damning consequences. Her unconscious turns back on her with a vengeance, as she suffers from debilitating migraine headaches. Terrified of anything beyond her control, Sybill

does not want to consult a psychiatrist: "Sybill regarded her unconscious like she regarded her reproductive system, as a messy, murky
darkness full of unexplained fluids and longings which she preferred
not to know too much about" (*Linen*, 17).

The similarly repressed mother in "Tongues of Fire" has enormous difficulty dealing with anything "below the belt":

> Mama referred to everything below the belt as "down there," an area she
> dealt with darkly, indirectly, and only when necessary. "Trixie Vopel is in the
> hospital for tests," she might say. "She's been having trouble 'down there.' "
> *Down there* was a foreign country, like Africa or Nicaragua. (*Eclipse*, 85)

Smith's imagination makes a connection that may reveal something
about the repressed, puritanical mind. The casting of peoples from
those lands that lie below the equator as sexual–sensual, dark,
moist, and hot–but not intelligent–mental, light, dry, and cold–is
based on a construction of the world's body that identifies what lies
below the equator with what lies "below the belt." Conversely, the
North Pole–pristine, snowy, white, cold–would be pure intellect,
untainted by all the murk that lies "down under." Sybill and Mama,
after all, are not just characters in stories but are types of females in
Smith's fiction who have caught the cultural sickness that females in
fact are supposed to catch to collude in the virgin/whore dichotomy.
If I am correct in my suspicion that Smith has put her finger on a cultural grid (i.e., equator = belt), it is easy to see why the snowy white
female would be equated with virginity (the Snow White syndrome)
and the dark lady with whoredom, as well as all sorts of other cultural biases equating southern lands with the sensual and northern
lands with the intellectual.[9]

Sybill cannot tolerate liminal places or things. She gets a migraine from just looking at the Peace rose, the way its colors run together. For her, all that matters is order, structure, and division.
There are no comings together or movings beyond. This horror of
commingling is concomitant to a horror of life itself. Sybill is closed;
she does not want anything to touch or penetrate her. Against
Sybill's will, the hypnotist in his gentle way ferrets out the truth:
Sybill is a virgin whose headaches begin when Ed Bing moves into
the condominium she manages, and she begins having unbidden
thoughts about him. Her reaction to seeing hairs in his sink during
an inspection betrays her inability to accept the reality of another

person, of another sex. Like Pearl, who wants everything to be pretty, Sybill refuses to enter human connection and human suffering.

Myrtle

Smith's fiction is a long exploration of the cost and the means of contact. It begins with self-knowledge, something Myrtle has used her family to shield herself from. She has "worked *hard* on herself" (*Linen,* 49) instead of learning anything about herself, and she congratulates herself that her 40 years do not show. She has managed to have an affair in which she feels nothing. Although Myrtle at least is active where Sybill is passive, she shares with Brooke and Crystal the sense of unreality: "Myrtle kept feeling like her life had happened to somebody else" (*Linen,* 61). She has been self-protective, but at 40 wishes she had allowed herself to feel more pain: "But somehow, since Mother had had a stroke, Myrtle wished she *had* [had her children by natural childbirth], she even wished she had felt all that pain [rather than being drugged when it happened]" (*Linen,* 61).

This thought is quickly followed by the kind of corrective cliché that Myrtle, like Richard Burlage, uses to keep from following her thoughts to a place she is afraid to explore. When she is close to the insight that allowing herself to feel pain would have given her the healing connection to her own experience, she fends off the insight by reassuring herself that at least she has protected herself from wear and tear. She meddles in her children's lives – one reason Sean is so angry is because, although their house is one of the biggest in town, he has no real privacy – but does not know them any better than she knows her husband, nor does she reveal herself to them. She is too distant from herself to do that. The couples and parenting courses are just superficial techniques: nothing is risked, nothing learned. With Gary, an exterminator and drifter, Myrtle reaches for the jolt of sensation, but there is no possibility of real contact there either. Like Monica with Buck Fire, Myrtle is just using Gary as a temporary relief from the boredom of a marriage she is not willing to take the necessary risks to change. Gary is 26, "really just a boy" (*Linen,* 54) who, again, she does not know any better than she knows her husband.

Myrtle likes Gary for his anonymity. He hardly seems to care enough to break her carefully constructed shell. She explains this to herself in one of her clichés, when she says to herself that Gary is "laid back" (*Linen*, 54). Because Gary does not exist in his own right, he serves to feed Myrtle's fantasies of a life she did not live:

Nothing was *wrong*, exactly, but she began to feel she was missing out – on what, she couldn't have told you.

. . . Myrtle missed the sixties entirely, while she was having babies. She used to hear the Beatles on the radio, that was about it. When she wasn't having babies, she was typing. She typed her way through the late sixties and early seventies. She never took part in a demonstration, or went to a big rock concert. She never knew anything that happened until she read about it in *Time*. She watched Vietnam and Watergate on TV, of course. But she never bought a pair of blue jeans before she was thirty. So she missed the whole thing. (*Linen*, 51)

Gary has no ambitions, goes to movies, drinks a lot of beer, smokes marijuana, wears old blue jeans and fish-net T-shirts: "Myrtle would not be caught dead with him" (*Linen*, 54). Gary is an experiment in the physical dimension of sexuality alone, a safe attempt to sample the other side of life without breaking through. Yet Myrtle seems to have picked someone she cannot hurt; as far as we know, she does not hurt Gary as Monica does Buck Fire.

Myrtle has grown up with an image of what traditional life should be, and she has accomplished it too well. Like so many of Smith's rigidly conventional characters, she is trapped in society's image and cannot imagine a way out. The image she works so hard to sustain was apparently first constructed by her image of her mother. Even in the stream of her thinking, Myrtle plies herself with all the platitudes. She and Don have "a marriage made in heaven" (*Linen*, 46); she loves him "with all her heart" (*Linen*, 48). The truth is that they do not know each other at all. Sean's rage is comprehensible; he is growing up in a house where no real feeling is expressed. Everyone is too busy soldiering on, looking respectable, just as Myrtle's mother, Miss Elizabeth, may have done when she hid the murder of her husband and raised her sister Fay's child by him as her own.

Myrtle is obsessed with appearances, and her every thought, about herself and others, is judgmental. Yet in this novel of forgiveness, this trait of Myrtle's is always bound up with her need to reassure herself that, in fact, she can live up to these judgments. When her half-sister, Candy, comes in to Miss Elizabeth's bedside, Myrtle's thoughts are judgmental in much the same way that Stella's are about her sister Florrie in "Cakewalk": "Candy came in then looking like a nurse herself in her white uniform. But she's *not* a nurse, she's a beautician. Actually she doesn't look like *that*, either—everything Candy wears looks exactly the same, like something she just threw on temporarily to run to the post office, not like anything you'd plan to wear all day" (*Linen*, 57-58).

But immediately Myrtle must reassure herself that at least she has on the right clothes. All Myrtle's thoughts at the bedside are self-absorbed, yet they also reveal her human frailty. As her mother dies, she tells Don, afraid to open the Pandora's box of her real feelings, that she has "mixed emotions" (*Linen*, 57). Because she finally cannot find herself and her feelings acceptable, Myrtle reaches out for a cliché, like "mixed emotions," and thus slays any hope of communication. She thinks how embarrassed and ashamed her mother would be to be seen like this—the same thing as not wanting to be found a suicide with your head in the oven (a concern of Joline Newhouse in Smith's short story "Between the Lines"). Yet it pleases her; she gloats. For she thinks none of them could ever satisfy her mother but Sybill. To buoy herself, she reminds herself how much better she is than Candy, how her mother gave up on Candy when she ran wild and got pregnant. Yet it troubles her "how well those kids of Candy's have turned out" (*Linen*, 58).

Don Dotson

In his role as husband and father, Don Dotson puts a label on everything too. He says Miss Elizabeth is "anal retentive and lives in a fantasy world" (*Linen*, 49). He pays lip service to "lifelong growth . . . constant flux and change" (*Linen*, 50), but having said it, he lets the aphorism circumvent the need for doing it. Myrtle and Don mistake language for reality. In their couples' communication course, in their parental active listening, they mistake the language for the act. Their idea of maturity is pseudomaturity, a controlled façade. Language becomes a mask; it replaces action and screens people from reality. Don and Myrtle work too hard to sustain their image of a marriage; there is no playfulness, no passion, no contact. They sustain each other's images and roles yet miss the point. If the purpose of a home is to maintain a place of real intimacy, where one can know and be known, Don and Myrtle have constructed an empty shell. They keep their lives circumspect; they avoid making a mess. To all appearances they have a perfect marriage, but the key word is *appearance*. If the beginning of wisdom is to know and love another human being, Don and Myrtle never get started.

Don has affinities with the willfully benign Manly Neighbors but is a more compassionately imagined character and is really a healer. Smith is gentle with Don, an orphan who wants so badly to have a normal life and can only imagine such a life by the book. (His orphan status groups him with the mythic figures in *Oral History*, whose origins are cloudy.) She shows compassion for this man trying too hard to live out an image of concerned family man. Under this artifice, she allows him to make a real connection. Like Claude in "Cakewalk" and the grandfather in "Artists," Don has found, outside his marriage, a woman he can touch. For 20 years he has been having an affair with Candy, Myrtle's sister. Yet this admittedly adulterous affair – with its potential to so damage a family – is, in this novel of reconciliation, almost an affirmation of family solidarity. Candy does not so much seem to be betraying her sister as filling in for what her sister cannot be. The affair is not tawdry or decadent; it is as deep and committed as a marriage, marked overall by mutual respect. Candy understands both Don's need to remain a family man and her own need for solitude and independence. It is, oddly, through Candy's eyes that we see Don's basic decency. Without her, he might appear to be nothing more than a pompous ass: "She's known other men, off and on. Don has never said a word, or minded. Well, how could he? But you know, deep down, he could. You know what men expect. Except for Don, who is different, who is a genuinely good man. He loves his wife and family, he works on it. He is a man who does right. Sometimes Candy thinks he works on it too hard" (*Linen*, 119).

Candy is able to comfort Don, who tells her that she is "the wild card in his deck" (*Linen*, 119). We see him best through her eyes. Candy tells Don to "hush" when he "gets into relating. . . . Expressing his feelings" (*Linen*, 120). Candy says, in more direct language, that the two of them are "like an old pair of shoes, real comfortable, back in the closet. Don's different here. Here, he says, he lets down his hair. He doesn't have to get ahead in the world, or figure anything out" (*Linen*, 119).

Candy

Candy is the center that *Black Mountain Breakdown* could never find. She is a reincarnation of Dory, but with the resources to survive. She is soft, but she is tough. When she talks to herself, it is direct. Her warm openness to life is the counterpoise to Sybill's rigidity and Myrtle's illusions. Candy sees things clearly and accepts them. She does not refuse to enter human suffering. At the dying woman's bedside, when Myrtle assumes that Miss Elizabeth must be embarrassed to be seen in such a state and would not want to be touched, Candy rushes in and takes her mother's hand. Candy responds to life. She is not thinking about how she looks, and she is not afraid to touch. Uncontrived, reaching out, she touches her dying mother.

In Candy Smith finds a character to affirm what she wants to affirm. Candy has generosity of spirit. Nonjudgmental, she accepts her own feelings and those of others. Smith sees Candy as the heroine of the novel, "the most important character to me – and the most successful, well-integrated person. She is the only one who lives successfully and works out her ideas and her aesthetics. She's very much her own person and the shaping force within the family, within the community."[10]

Candy is honest with herself and life and tolerates pain. She cries as she finishes preparation of Miss Elizabeth's body. Candy is also a counterbalance to the victimization of Fay, as well as of Crystal of *Black Mountain Breakdown* and Dory of *Oral History*. Perhaps more than any other Smith character, we can trust her voice. Candy is a mythic ennoblement of what society would see as sweet, transitory, and pleasurable, the very way in which women are so often labeled, marginalized, and trivialized. Smith makes this woman the center and the strength of life's noble quest. Again crossing boundaries and exploding expectations, Smith often uses the diminutive form of female names (two syllables ending in *y*, recalling Faulkner's Caddy) – Dory, Lily, Ivy, Candy, Sandy, Lacy, names that culture has trivialized – for her strongest and most complex characters.

Lacy

It remains to Lacy to complete the struggle of Brooke and Crystal to achieve authenticity through language. Lacy, too, confronts pain: "Lacy was never prepared for the pain that kept coming over her:

pain so bitter it was sweet almost, like a sore tooth which you have
to keep touching with your tongue" (*Linen*, 69). It is Lacy who discovers and cherishes her mother's journal and remembers the small
book of poetry her mother wrote. She thinks, as do Myrtle and Sybill,
that she, more so than her siblings, is really her mother's daughter:

> I am her daughter, in a sense, more than the others: more than Sybill, than
> Myrtle, certainly more than Candy. I am more her daughter in a way she could
> never understand, since I look, I suppose, so different; and since with her,
> appearances are everything. But the poetry *took*, with me. And how very
> strange, since she could never tell good from bad, poor thing, or see beyond
> the iron pink palace of niceness and illusion, of should and sweet, which she
> had constructed around all of us. She never knew any of us, really. I wonder if
> she ever knew Daddy, or anybody. Anybody at all. I wonder now if anyone
> ever does – and if we do, if it's worth it, all the trouble and pain, when it
> doesn't last. (*Linen*, 69)

Thus Lacy is seen to be honestly grappling with the problems of
pain, loss, and illusion that beset so many of Smith's characters. She,
too, has constructed illusions, and she begins to sort them out as she
deals with her mother's death. She realizes that her quest for saint-
hood, like the structure of her marriage, has been too contrived.
What is required for both, she realizes, is human empathy and human passion. She thinks, "All that good will and the mutual interests
and ideals that seemed to be so important, and seem to her now to
be inconsequential. Better a blind obsession, better a fascination
with the nape of somebody's neck" (*Linen*, 162). Lacy realizes that
with Jack she has been living in a shell: "It was Jack's shell; Jack had
made it and made her, fashioned her, too, in a way, but now Jack
was gone. *It's worse to be abandoned if you were first rescued.*
Then you have nothing left except a void. Empty space. Lacy felt
raw, exposed, vulnerable. She could not seem to get her bearings"
(*Linen*, 70). Sally in *Oral History* was also married to a man who
wanted to "save" her.

By the novel's end, Lacy does get her bearings. She is recon-
structing a relationship with Jack, the father of her two children. Jack
is still living with the graduate student for whom he abandoned her,
but he and Lacy have dinner together on Thursday nights. She does
not know what will happen, but it seems that, with Jack or not, she

has some sense of balance in her life. For Lacy, as for the other characters, there seems to be hope.

A Joyous Baptism

Family Linen marks an enormous step forward in Smith's work; it shows redemption for the family. Fay finds release in death, enclosed in the hot car, believing that Jewell Rife is finally taking her on the trip he promised her. Myrtle has driven out to Gary's house, seen the disorder, and fled. To everyone's surprise, she agrees to leave the suburbs and move back with Don into the ancestral family home. The present has found a healing reconnection with the past. Don assumes the role of *paterfamilias,* as Candy knew he would, taking care of things because he cares. In many ways, Don has acted the role of healer: allaying Sybill's fears in making confirmation of her story possible, providing for the family pool, insisting on the return to the ancestral home. Myrtle and Don prepare for the marriage of their daughter, Karen, now pregnant by a brilliant computer expert, in a way that seems to ensure continuity and joy, providing for both tradition and individual expression:

> But Don wanted Karen to have a proper start in life, he believes in that, and his heart swelled to bursting when he walked her around the side of the pool to where Karl stood with that young Episcopal rector whose name he can never remember but who certainly knows how to do things right. Of course Don wishes they had stuck to the prayerbook, but once Karen and Karl gave in to the idea of a wedding at all, Don didn't quibble. And the poem Theresa wrote for the occasion was pretty enough, although Kate and Lacy told Myrtle it was "sappy." Well, why not? This is not Chapel Hill. This is Booker Creek, where Don and Myrtle will live for the rest of their lives in this house on the hill at the end of town, and even Myrtle likes it now. (*Linen,* 266)

Myrtle agrees to let Karen make her wedding dress out of one of Miss Elizabeth's old lace tablecloths, if Karen promises not to tell anyone except the family (*Linen,* 268). If Brooke's family had been able to allow this kind of originality and individual expression, where family traditions were renewed instead of used to stifle, family and community rituals would have healed Brooke's inner and outer self, instead of splitting them irrevocably. In any case, Karen – who looks pretty and dimpled in her pregnancy – makes her wedding dress out of the family linen. She is beautiful.

Sean has achieved a reconciliation with his father, who he knows is right and good, even if his language is false. Sean and his father both cry when Sean actually shoots himself with his grandfather's gun. Sybill has been proved sane, and even she feels proud and needed at the wedding: "She likes the urgency of a wedding, the intricacy of the timing, the general need for some precision all around. Which she, thank God, has been able to supply!" (*Linen*, 268).

Arthur has found some hope with his mother's nurse, Mrs. Palucci, and her son Buddy, which makes him feel reconnected to his girls: "Arthur thinks it would be interesting to hang around this kid, Buddy, and watch him grow up. There ought to be some interesting moments, over the years. Arthur thinks of his own girls, that he loves so, and kisses Mrs. Palucci behind the boxwood" (*Linen*, 270). Clinus puts up a sign on his billboard: "KAREN AND KARL, TODAY IS THE FIRST DAY OF THE REST OF YOUR LIFE" (*Linen*, 272). With a new spirit of reconciliation, the author remarks, "That goes for everybody" (*Linen*, 272).

Best of all, some sort of impulse takes hold of the inebriated bride and groom and wedding guests: "Tomorrow, nobody will remember exactly who was the first one in the pool, but soon it's full of churning bodies, pale flashing flesh beneath the water" (*Linen*, 272). The wedding at the end is in sharp contrast to the wedding at the end of *Something in the Wind*. At the end of *Family Linen*, the whole, happy, inebriated crowd dives into the swimming pool, built on the site of the family well that held the bones of the murdered patriarch. It is a joyous baptism. It is a moment when tradition, religion, and family are simultaneously redeemed by a southern woman's salvific imagination. It may be Lee Smith's most joyous moment in print. Certainly, in a redemptive moment, Lacy, the inheritor of Lee Smith's struggle with memory, language, and loss, recovers her own memory: "Strange that Lacy can't remember . . . the Dodd boy, at the lake, especially since he was sweet on her. But then suddenly Lacy has an idea of him, outlined against the blue water, braced against the pull of the rope, his bright open face a shining blur in the rushing wind" (*Linen*, 272).

Chapter Seven

A New, Authoritative Voice:
Fair and Tender Ladies

The Music That Breathes

The seed for *Fair and Tender Ladies* was sown when Smith bought a packet of letters for 75 cents at a yard sale and found the letters to contain a woman's whole life in correspondence to her sister. It occurred to Smith that if the writer of the letters "had a chance to be educated and not have five children she might have really been a writer of some note" (Ringle, F6). The letter writer in Smith's novel is the redheaded Ivy Rowe. Although Ivy writes many different people, the most significant letters are to her beautiful, silvery sister, Silvaney.

A brain fever damages Silvaney's mind; the murder of her twin brother, Babe, destroys it. A do-gooder, meddling in mountain culture, has Silvaney institutionalized. She is placed in a home for lunatics, where she dies in the flu epidemic after World War I. The twins appear to symbolize two sides of the unsocialized self necessary for imagination but displaced, and really at risk, in society. By refusing to believe Silvaney is dead, continuing to write her, Ivy apparently keeps that side of herself alive – "my lost one, my heart" (*Fair*, 120).

Until her own death, Ivy never stops writing Silvaney; she will not abandon her, not ever. In effect, this is the rescue of that part of the female spirit imaged (and imaged as damaged) in Crystal, Lily, Dory, Pearl, and Fay. This primal she, silver-haired like she was "fotched up on the moon," is now the muse, a mountain sylph, the internal self, a wood spirit, forever running wild and free: "I will tell you of my Family now and she will be first, I love Silvaney the

bestest, you see. Silvaney is so pretty, she is the sweetest. . . . She
takes after a Princess in a story, Silvaney does" *(Fair,* 17).

> She scares easy, sometimes she will put her apron up over her head and start
> in crying and other times she will get to laghing and she cant stop, you have
> to pour a gourdfull of water down over her face. . . . Silvaney is bigger and
> oldern me, but it is like we are the same sometimes it is like we are one. We
> have slept in the same bed all of our lives and done everything as one. I am
> smart thogh I go to school when I can and try to better myself and teach Sil-
> vaney but she cant learn. . . . We put black-eye susans and Queen Annes lace
> in our hair. *(Fair,* 17)

As with *Oral History,* Smith used research on Appalachia (which
she published at the back of the book) for this epistolary novel that
"spans four generations, three wars (Ivy's grandson goes to Vietnam), the gradual, sad loss of a way of life, and the entire range of
human experience. It is a novel about Appalachia, family, forgiveness, love and the resilience of the spirit."[1]

Those critics who had expressed disappointment that *Family
Linen* did not measure up to "the myth-laden, haunted lushness of a
Black Rock, a Hoot Owl Holler" found *Fair and Tender Ladies* a
novel that makes the mythic present, the present mythic, and is
"drunk on the language of Appalachia."[2] In fact, *Fair and Tender
Ladies* brings together male and female, female and female, body and
mind, collective and individual, art and love, as does the figure and
function of Aphrodite, "the music that breathes" (Friedrich, 220),
the inspirer of love, longing, and poetry. Smith breathes into this
novel the lyricism of a woman's life, gives it the dignity and durability
of collective language – renders it mythic. On its release the novel
was variously described as "a mixture of lyricism and sexual boldness that might have been sung into being" *(Newsweek,* 72H) and
"as true to life as the high, sweet sound of mountain music in a gathering dusk" (Kinsella, 9).

Oral History was the turning point. Smith wrote her way out of
social constraints and patriarchy. She lifted the problems of her female protagonists out of isolated selves and made them public and
collective. She tapped or recreated (it matters not which) "the secret
stream, below ground, of our classical heritage of symbolic communication."[3] Golden Dory must be sacrificed for the Secret
Wound – the split between culture and nature, male and female,

body and soul–ultimately, the split between sacred and sexual. Society finally turns Dory into the quintessential female by severing her
head from her body: she could not do this to herself spiritually, as
had Brooke and Crystal, so she allowed society's machine to do it for
her physically. The same culture turns the Victor of *Oral History* into
the quintessential male. He has the head with no body. He is the
voice of abstraction in the library, whiling away his hours with disembodied ideas on flat pages, with no golden Dorys to trouble his
cognitive renderings.

This is not the case in *Fair and Tender Ladies*. With a Herculean
feat of integration, Smith returns to her territory–the mountains and
the conflict–and finally writes her way to another end, one that no
longer demands the death of the female. She has imagined her way
out of the accepted social construction. Through imagination and
written form, Lee Smith has made that other end publicly available
for females and collectively compelling. She has given us an authoritative voice that sings another story.

The Authorial Voice

"Authoritative" is what was called for. In Smith's earlier fiction, the
silencing (*Black Mountain Breakdown*), ignoring ("Saint Paul,"
"The Seven Deadly Sins," "I Dream of Horses"), and even removal
of the actual female is imaged time and again, and when the root
cause is traced, it leads back to mythic cultural foundations. The removal of the actual female is imaged in Smith's short story "Not Pictured," when another of her golden women, the lovely Lily, is put
away in a mental hospital. Lily's name evokes both Judeo-Christian
and non-Judeo-Christian mythology and alludes to erasure of women
in received myth. Lily echoes Lilith–the powerful, sexual, sacred female who was "put away" in Judeo-Christian mythology. Furthermore, "the apple was the main symbol of the Baltic Sun Maiden,
the pomegranate and lily of the Ishtars, and the rose of the Indo-
European dawn. ('Two great classes of flora are paired with two aspects of love in woman')" (Friedrich, 75). Additionally, the early
Sidonians worshiped a sensuous Astarte (or Asherah?), "depicted as
a naked woman in the prime of her years, often with emphasis on the

erotic zones. The lily that she held symbolized her charm, the serpent her fecundity" (Friedrich, 18).

In the desecration of both the apple of the Baltic Sun Maiden and the serpent of Astarte, and in the reassigning of the lily, we witness the same phenomenon, the root cause: the defiling of women and the symbols of their power. Arguably, had Mary Magdalene's role been taken into account, Easter symbolism need not have so obliterated female in exchange for male transcendent, regenerative power. For it is Magdalene who comes to the tomb while it is still dark the third day after the crucifixion, the sexual woman in the dark, just before dawning. It is Magdalene who sees the angels, Magdalene to whom Christ first appears and gives the charge of telling the disciples that he is not dead, but risen. This sacred task goes to Magdalene – the sacred, sexual, active female – who asks the man she believes to be the gardener to tell her where they have taken the body of her lord and "I will take him away" (John 20:15). The active female, she will go and get him. It is Magdalene whose name Jesus calls and she who recognizes his voice and says, "Rabboni" (teacher). It is Magdalene who sees and conveys, and thus gives transcendent birth, not just to flesh but to spirit. It is she who brings the message that spirit is here, with us.

Christian iconography has not recognized the goddess of the dawn, who brings forth the resurrected sun, but Christ did. And Lee Smith, who gets it all and treats it all with humor, puts Mary Magdalene in *Fair and Tender Ladies:* "I would rate that Little Garnie Rowe about average as a preacher, and I'd bet furthermore that a lot of his fame has come from those that travel with him, such as Little Mary Magdalene in her pink dress, and this other young man that calls himself John Three Sixteen with a real deep singing voice" (*Fair*, 257). But it not the active sexual female who is honored in Christian iconography; she is dishonored. In *Fair and Tender Ladies* she is diminished, "little," and in a pink dress, not full and red.

This whole cultural drift is sadly apparent in the case of Lilith, whose name Lily's echoes:

> Another figure who conjoins sex and sadism is Lilith. She first appears as a Sumerian she-demon, roughly contemporary with Inanna (and mentioned about 2400 B.C.). She is beautiful but barren, a vampire and a harlot. She is still present in the late Babylonian period and was probably well known to the Hebrews, although she is mentioned only once (Isaiah 34:14). She becomes

much more important in the Talmudic and, even more in the Kabbalistic period. By this time she is often nude, sexually aggressive, a child-killer, liminal,
very red (lips, hair, robe), and the procreatress of a whole race of demons. In
some ways, but only some, the medieval Hebrews distinguished sharply between two aspects of sensuousness (roughly Eve versus Lilith) that had been
fused in Cybele, Astarte, and even some of the Greek Aphrodites. This distinction corresponds roughly to the one in many contemporary cultures between
a wife and a whore (i.e., *either* a wife *or* a whore). . . . Some variant of the
Babylonian goddess was seen by the authors of Revelation 17 as a woman
with whom the kings of the earth had fornicated "and the inhabitants of the
earth have been made drunk with the wine of her fornication. . . . A woman
upon a scarlet-colored beast, full of the names of blasphemy, having seven
heads and ten horns . . . arrayed in purple and scarlet color, and decked with
gold and precious stones and pearls, and having a golden cup in her hand full
of abominations and the filthiness of her fornication." (Friedrich, 213)

"I Dream of Horses" is another short story that chronicles the loss of
female mythology and concomitant loss of understanding female
psychology.

Ivy Rowe's is the healing, authorial voice *both* telling and writing
a new story, inserting her story into the canon as well as speaking
the mother tongue. Growing up in the mountains, Ivy *writes* in
mountain dialect, thus providing a bridge between the lyrical oral
and the codified written. Her first rhapsodic letters are set against no
standard English that would tarnish and diminish their magic power.
Some readers and critics expressed disappointment that her language became more standardized over time, but that may simply be a
part of Ivy's learning to live both lyrically and realistically in the
world. Ivy Rowe, whose name promises culture that does not deal
the death blow to nature, is born around the turn of the century, the
time of the first Almarine's manhood. Her life spans both world wars
and Vietnam, but the mythic past is also present. When Ivy and
Honey Breeding – both exactly the same size, like Red Emmy and Almarine and Dory and Richard – make love on a mountaintop and in a
cave, Ivy asserts that "Whitebear Whittington lives yet up on Hell
Mountain. . . . He lives there now I tell you and he is wild, wild. He
runs throgh the night with his eyes on fire and no one can take him,
yet he will sleep of a day as peaceful as a lullaby" (*Fair,* 315).

We are as far back in time as Red Emmy (Ivy, too, is redheaded),
as man's earliest religious stirrings, when the goddess of the hearth
sat and talked all night with the cave bear, the "earliest animal mas-

ter" (Campbell 1987a, 349). According to Campbell, the cave-bear
sanctuaries date from ca. 200,000 to 25,000 B.C. (1987a, 395), putting
us back in time before the diminishment and eventual defilement of
the naked goddess and her replacement by men in magical cos-
tumes.[4] So in some sense we jump the gap jumped in *Oral History*,
going all the way back to an imagined time before the devolution of
the female image occurred, before Inanna became the whore of
Babylon.

But the sacred-sexual figure of Ivy, bridging as she does the present and the mythic past, heals this split. Smith seems again, by *Fair
and Tender Ladies*, to associate caves with female sexuality. The first
time Ivy is kissed – by her future husband, Oakley Fox – is when as a
girl she has entered a cave in a timid exploration (*Fair*, 59). She goes
back to stand at the cave mouth after his death.

Furthermore, Ivy has a mind, but it is not a disembodied mind.
Even though she is a reader and a writer, she is not a "disembodied
voice in the library"; the book is epistolary, woman's immanent
thought and art. Ivy refuses all the lures and rewards of the dominant culture, including a Boston education and European travel, and
chooses to stay in her beloved mountains. She refuses to be condemned by polite culture: pregnant and unmarried, she is glad to be
"ruint" because it makes her free. She refuses to be condemned by
the church, closing her mind to hell-fire-and-brimstone preacher,
Brother Garnie, who tells her that she is Babylon's "whore and an
abomination" (*Fair*, 251). And Ivy never abandons Silvaney, that part
of the female self that is all shimmering, vulnerable light and tenderness, who, because society is so cruel to it, must be hidden in the
silvery part of the imagination. Silvaney's name evokes woodland
spirits – the maenads and satyrs, wilderness companions of Bacchus,
who abandoned themselves in sheer ecstasy to the joys of wine and
dance. *Satyr and Maenad,* a portion of a Roman frieze at New York's
Metropolitan Museum of Art, is a paean to wild joy worthy of Silvaney herself. Yet further corroborative proof of the desacralizing of
female joy is evidenced by *Webster's* dictionary, which glosses satyr
as "a wildnerness god" but maenad as "a madwoman."

Ivy writes Silvaney, even after Silvaney is dead. As Smith's writing
becomes more healing, she gives wounded women each other; she
gives them sisters who bring self-repair. Ivy goes the final step and
takes this damaged and beloved figure inside, as part of herself, part

of her psychic core, and refuses to allow her to die. Society kills her, but the point now becomes quite different from Smith's earlier novels, in which the woman had needed to learn to admit that death existed but also that they need not be complicitous to societal murder. When society has killed something so valuable, the point is for women, humans, to keep it alive, even if only in the imagination. Ivy refuses to admit that Silvaney is dead, even after her brother Victor – the second Victor in Smith's fiction who is a voice for cynicism and negation – throws Silvaney's death in her face. Here, by refusing to admit it, Ivy is keeping Silvaney alive and hence making that part of women's lives durable. Ivy has what Crystal Spangler lacked: a collective voice, a stubborn will, and a self-determination remade daily. Having made women's lives and their pain durable and collective – that is, mythic – in *Fair and Tender Ladies* Smith can allow them imaginative flight.

Aphrodite and Demeter

Perhaps some future titan of the novel or epic will create a full synthesis of the meanings of Demeter and Aphrodite that will recapture the archaic synthetic imagery of the early Mayans and Indo-Europeans. Perhaps, also, we can hope for a future that will recognize, accept, and encourage the deep and natural connections between sexuality and motherliness-maternity. The split between them should be healed in the world view, or by the religion, by the system of ideas, whatever it is called, that connects our concrete lives with the awesome powers beyond our control. (Friedrich, 191)

With *Fair and Tender Ladies* we come to the fulfillment of our long exploration of the problem of female development in Smith's fiction. Ivy Rowe, whose name promises order without destruction of nature, embodies female victory over the social forces, externally inflicted and internally realized, that would destroy her. This novel stands in direct counterpoise to *Black Mountain Breakdown*, with *Oral History's* sacrificial offering of Dory the mediating link. Arguably, *Fair and Tender Ladies* solves what Friedrich sees as the greatest single problem in female psychological development: the disjunction of sex-sensuousness and maternity-motherliness or, as he argues it is embodied, the separation of Aphrodite and Demeter

(Friedrich, 187-88). Dory had embodied Aphrodite and Demeter, and Dory died. She found herself in the same position as Anna Karenina in more ways than one: "Anna Karenina certainly houses the two complexes [Aphrodite and Demeter] within herself, but it is precisely the conflicts they engender that lead to her suicide" (Friedrich, 183). When we recall the cat, Anna Karen, in Smith's first novel, we see that this was always a preoccupation: " 'It's named for a Russian lady Mama told me about, who got killed when a train ran over her. That's how much you know about anything.' Gregory was mad. He walked off and the cat went after him. I liked that cat a whole lot more after I knew about the Russian lady and the train. I wondered why she didn't run when she saw that train coming at her" (*Last*, 9).

The lady did not run because she had internalized the split. Friedrich traces the disjunction of these emotional complexes – sex-sensuousness and maternity-motherliness – as far back as Inanna: "One decisive fact is that Inanna is never maternal, and that procreation and generation are patronized by various important mother goddesses, with whom she should not be confused. . . . The sharp dichotomization between sexuality and maternity anticipates at the very outset of this study a basic issue" (Friedrich, 14). Friedrich sees Aphrodite as a synthesis: she is not only the most sensual and powerful but the most motherly of the four queens of heaven – Hera, Athena, Aphrodite, and Artemis. But in his analysis her motherliness and maternity is relegated to secondary status, and "the symbolic conflicts between this and sexuality/sensuousness" keep her from filling what he refers to as an "emotional gap" in the Greek pantheon (Friedrich, 150). He sees Demeter as standing for the mother-child bond, especially the bond between mother and daughter:

> It is the Greek Demeter, the loving, nurturing, grieving mother, who alone can be said to epitomize the tenderness and loyalty between mother and daughter, which reaches a sort of acme during the daughter's later childhood and early adolescence – precisely when Persephone [the daughter] was raped. [Demeter] stands for motherliness just as Aphrodite stands for sensuousness, and in each case the meaning is partly Greek and partly universal. (Friedrich, 158)

But Friedrich goes on to note that the filling of the "emotional gap" by Demeter still leaves a lacuna in integrated female psychology. The dichotomy between erotic and maternal remains (and we are back to the starting point of *The Last Day the Dogbushes Bloomed*), even when all the queens of heaven are explored: "Both Aphrodite and Athena lack a mother (in some sense), but one incarnates sexuality while the other is a- or antisexual. Artemis is antisexual but is maximally identified with her mother (and in earlier myth was very much a mother figure herself). It is striking that nowhere, even when we add Demeter-Persephone, is a strong mother tie combined with strongly positive sexuality" (Friedrich, 160). In surveying "myth, religion, and high literature" Friedrich finds the dissociation of sex-sensuousness and maternity-motherliness a barrier against "a more general image of the artistically creative woman" (Friedrich 182, 190). The separation of emotional complexes that no doubt derive from the same source prevents a woman from being understood or from understanding herself.[5]

Synthesis

Ivy Rowe walks out of this conflict and establishes a different option, another ending. Society and its cultural imagings continue to be destructive of her self, but she is not. Ivy constitutes a synthesis of Aphrodite and Demeter, incorporating both in her person and in her life. She balances these impulses and refuses the prescriptions of patriarchy – shame, self-disgust – by staying close to her mountain roots, her womanly life. She is, to borrow Friedrich's words, "at once maternal, sororal, and erotic" (Friedrich, 46), intelligent and proud.

With Honey Breeding, a beekeeper whose name and occupation suggest a union of male and female, of sweet sexuality and equality between honey men and candy women, we have come as far from the rape of Susan and of Crystal as possible. Honey Breeding's name also means a union of nature and culture. Smith has given us a new sex god and sex goddess, and we like them. As male and female get closer together, they become more alike in size and in essence. In fact, Honey Breeding becomes like Aphrodite: "He is not a big man, Silvaney. . . . He is skinny, wiry, with pale thick curly gold hair on his forehead and thick gold eyebrows that nearabout grow together, and hair all over him like spun gold on his folded forearms. . . . [He] did not seem quite real. He seemed more like a woods creature fetched up somehow from the forest, created out of fancy, on a whim" (*Fair*, 214).[6]

As the 40-year-old mother of five children, Ivy surrenders to sensuality with Honey Breeding. Like Joline B. Newhouse of the short story "Between the Lines," with her memory of Marcel Wilkes in the "holy Woods," Ivy never regrets this affair. She feels it brings her back to life, gives her her "soul back," and renews her relationship with her husband. But, as with Joline, there is some struggle with the idea of punishment, of inflicting suffering on children. Joline struggles but finally refuses to believe that her son's birth defect is a result of her "sin." Ivy comes down from the mountain to find that her next-to-youngest daughter, LuIda, is dead, apparently from an attack of appendicitis (*Fair*, 250). Ivy says that "a part of me died with her" (*Fair*, 243) and, further, "I know LuIda's dying is all my fault and if I had not run off with Honey Breeding it would not have happened, LuIda would be alive today, playing down at the creek from Maudy. . . . I wish it was me instead" (*Fair*, 244).

Ivy does not receive Joline's consolation, but Ivy nonetheless never repudiates the joy of her time with Honey Breeding, nor does she put herself in the way of any trains. The anxiety of the disjunction, however, is not erased, for the death of LuIda encodes the conflict between sex-sensuousness and maternity-motherliness. But men, too, are not free from this disjunction. As characters, Ivy's uncle Revel Rowe, her lover Franklin Ransom, and even Honey Breeding are subjected to stereotyping in which "a large number of women in many cultures dichotomize men just as sharply into what is a mirror image of the lover versus the mother; into the sensuous (and relatively irresponsible) male lover versus the positive and nurturing father-husband" (Friedrich, 188). Honey's configuration as liminal and a divinity, however, may take him beyond such categories. In some ways, Honey and Oakley Fox may be seen as personifications of the dichotomy. But the larger issue here is the split between sacred and profane.

The interlude with Honey Breeding is necessary for Ivy to feel alive enough to give life to her children. It is a moment of sacred sex, of healing the Secret Wound. This moment intersects with a timeless realm and bestows, at least temporarily, divinity. It seems to be an encounter with the divine – the moment of sacred sex being

what we call god – and thus beyond the categories of social stereotypes.

Ivy's Family

Ivy's first letters show a strong identification with the mother. Like
Pricey Jane, Ivy observes the effects of a hard life on her mother who
becomes "hard as a rocky-clift, and her eyes burns out in her head"
(*Fair,* 27). "My momma was young and so pretty when she come
riding up Sugar Fork, but she does not look pretty now, she looks
awful, like her face is hanted, she has had too much on her" (*Fair,*
15). She also writes lovingly of Granny Rowe, who "chews tobaccy
and spits in the fire" (*Fair,* 21). The fact that "Granny Rowe is my
antie I think not my granny relly" (*Fair,* 21) does not diminish the
fact that Ivy remembers Granny's wisdom and advice throughout her
life, and even thinks she sees her, walking up ahead, at times of
trouble.

Women's relationships with women are much more fully developed in *Fair and Tender Ladies* than in Smith's other novels. They
are teaching, talking to, telling stories about, and connecting to other
women. Granny's sister, Tennessee, is a sort of Aphrodite-gone-to-
seed who exposes herself to men. Ivy also loves the old sisters,
Gaynelle and Virgie Cline, who arrive on "Old Christmas! for this is
when they used to come every year, January 5 like clockwork and
stay up all nigt and drink coffee and tell storys with Daddy, they did
it when he was not but a child living here with his own momma and
daddy and his sister Vicey and brother Revel. Daddy allus said it
seemed to him that they were old ladys then, so dont nobody know
how old they migt be now" (*Fair,* 33). It is the Cline sisters who tell
the mythic story of Whitebear Whittington. Later, with Honey
Breeding, Ivy says she is "starved for stories," stories told by wise,
craggy, and sometimes tender old women.

Ivy also has tender regard for her father, whom she mostly
knows as lying on a "pallet" with a heart condition but remembers
as healthy, saying to her: *"Farming is pretty work. . . . Now Ivy, this
is how spring tastes. This is the taste of spring"* (*Fair,* 42, 177). In
fact, there is healing in the father-male image in *Fair and Tender
Ladies,* partly signified by Ivy's father's name, John Arthur. This is the

third time the name Arthur appears in Smith's fiction. As Jean
Markale traces in *Women of the Celts*, the legendary Arthur "is a
mocked and cuckolded king whose wife Guinevere (Gwenhwyfar in
Welsh, meaning 'white shadow') symbolises true sovereignty according to Celtic belief; but she is often taken away from him by her
lovers and it is not unreasonable to wonder whether Arthur is a
later, patriarchal transformation of an ancient bear goddess"
(Markale, 92-93).

I realize that all the associations here cannot be disentangled
within the scope of this study. What I do wish to point out is how
Smith's imagination, and particularly her linguistic sense, restlessly
returns to root sources of cultural constructs that have to do with
white/black, female/male, and human/animal. If the name Arthur
does come from perhaps an animal and perhaps a female deity (the
postulated root of Celtic *arto-* yields "bear" and "Arthur"), then all
the boundaries drawn by patriarchal constructions – reified in heroic
tales of such semihistorical figures as Arthur – are breached.

What is important in *Fair and Tender Ladies* is that linguistic
possibilities merge with imaginative contents, and within Smith's
own naming and image system enormous reconciliation has occurred. The Arthur of *Fair and Tender Ladies* is a far cry from the
sick fantasy figure of Smith's first novel, *The Last Day the Dogbushes
Bloomed*. This Arthur is a tender and sensual man who teaches his
daughter how spring tastes and how pretty farming is. He is sick, but
what ails him is his heart – perhaps the best we can hope for of the
patriarch at this stage of Smith's work. And the figure that fires the
imagination in *Fair and Tender Ladies* is not the perverse Little
Arthur but a healthy animal – the wild Whitebear Whittington, who
runs through the night with his eyes on fire, and no one can take
him. Through Ivy's healthy imagination, the father and the animal are
held in tension, reconciled and redeemed. I am suggesting that one
reason this feels so satisfying is that Smith's unerring linguistic sense
has rediscovered an ancient connection.

To bridge domains further, Whitebear lives up on Hell Mountain.
(Hell fire probably stands for internal creative fire in the first place.)
As much as King Dog, who comes down from the mountaintop with
his 12 disciples to surround Susan in a healing vision, the image of
Whitebear Whittington, running Hell Mountain at night, redeems
darkness, fire, and even hell. John Arthur's red hair and his lying in

front of the fire while his heart hurts suggest both a kinship with the bear and the possible source of his heart trouble. Now Smith, who had refused to turn her back on Little Arthur in her first novel, nurses an Arthur neither perverse like Little Arthur nor trivialized like the Arthur of *Family Linen* (who in fact marries a nurse); this Arthur is a worthy man whose suffering hurts his daughter, and hurts us as well. John Arthur bears the Secret Wound (as does Crystal's father) – that iconography for the split between nature and culture, between matter and spirit, which Smith is trying to heal.

Although the father in *The Last Day the Dogbushes Bloomed* is not king in the way that the King Dog is, John Arthur of *Fair and Tender Ladies* may well be the bear. We can learn something about the imagination if we remember, as James Joyce in *Ulysses* reminds every English literature student, that "dog" is "god" spelled backwards. As Smith matured as a writer, her early crude playfulness with language – imaged in Susan's spellings and Brooke's crossword puzzles and practiced in "King Dog" – has developed into the ability to cast a spell as well as to discover those ancient crossroads where words – and meanings and categories usually held as oppositional – really do intersect, making it possible for us to remake the world. Reversal and sarcasm are liberating, but they do not heal like the slow and painful digging for forgotten connections.

Maternal Instincts

Ivy likes the mothering duties she has as one of many children ("The next leastest has to watch out for the leastest ones, and I loved to do that" [*Fair*, 19]), and she becomes a mother herself at about age 18. Mothering, or at least a choice of heterosexual love that leads to mothering, is what she chooses instead of going to Boston with Miss Torrington to "fulfill her potential." Miss Torrington's sudden and passionate kiss on the back of Ivy's neck seems to decide her against it.

Ivy stays in Majestic, Virginia. That very night, she has intercourse with Lonnie Rash. She does not love Lonnie Rash and does not pretend, even to herself, that she does. They are incompatible; he can neither read nor write, and Ivy is smart and knows it. He is simply the first male to whom she feels erotically drawn. Smith ac-

knowledges the need to address the purely erotic, but she sees it for
what it is. Even though Ivy is "ruint" she never thinks of marrying
him (he is eventually killed in World War I). When Lonnie leaves to
join the army, Ivy stands on the river bridge and watches the water
in "little eddies, little whirlpools." "Well, I thought, that's that, and
with him gone it was like my whole self came rushing back to me
again and I looked at the water and thought, Oh I *do* want to go to
Boston, I do want to go after all!" (*Fair*, 119). Her next thought is
particularly interesting in light of our discussion of emotional disjunction: "And I recalled Miss Torringtons letter, how she said that
there are kinds and kinds of love and that sometimes we confuse
them being only mortal as we are, and how she said that she would
never be other than my good true friend if I would reconsider coming" (*Fair*, 119).

Just as she is writing Miss Torrington to tell her she will come to
Boston, Ivy discovers her pregnancy, does not go to Boston, and
winds up going to Diamond to live with her eldest sister, Beulah,
who has delivered an illegitimate son and named him John Arthur,
just after their father's death. "Granny Rowe says that sometimes it
happens like that, one spirrit goes and a nother one comes direckly"
(*Fair*, 50). Ivy goes to live with Beulah and her husband, Curtis (who
finally marries Beulah against his mother's wishes), in Diamond
Mining's company town. Beulah is bitter about her past, her womanhood, her childbearing, and her red hair: "Dont you *ever*, Beulah
said, I mean *ever* Ivy Rowe, call old Granny over here with all her
crazy old ideas. I wont have it. I will not. Beulah laid in the bed with
her red hair splayed out on the pillow like a sunset. She is very beautiful. *I will not forget, she said, how we lived on Sugar Fork, how I
bore that one* – she pointed at John Arthur, playing with a pan on the
floor – *by myself on a cornhusk tick and cut the cord myself with
the hatchet*" (*Fair*, 134).

But Ivy's experience is different. Granny Rowe shows up just at
the time Ivy's baby, Joli, is to be born: "Then Beulah popped up and
said, Why that is ridiculous, Granny! You know nobody can tell exactly when a baby is coming, especially a first baby" (*Fair*, 143). "But
Granny laughed, and in the dark you could see her pipe shine red
[note the repetition of the color red] when she pulled on it. *It's the
full moon, honey, she said. Just look at it*" (*Fair*, 143).

Ivy's memory of the birth is lyrical, reversing Susan's fear and shame of the blood bucket:

> The blood smell was not so bad. It was sweet some way, it was not like anything else in the world, and now it will always be mixed up in my mind somehow with the moonlight and my baby, for then Granny handed her to me. I held her close by my side and looked at the moonlight on closest star [quilt]. . . . *This is important, I want to remember this, it is all so important, this is happening to me.* And I am so glad to write it down lest I forget. I lay there real still while the moonlight slowly crossed my quilt, and listened to a hoot owl off in the woods, and little Joli breathing, and – come morning – the long sweet whistle of the train. (*Fair,* 149)

The train no longer causes death; its sweet whistle we hear. And the woman herself – bleeding and red – has through Ivy's birthing and Smith's writing been redeemed. Ivy retains a special love for her firstborn all through her life, writing her in 1945: "And you can rest assured that there never was a daughter in this wide world that brought more joy to her mother's heart" (*Fair,* 268). Not only is Ivy happy to have Joli, but she is glad she is "ruint" because it saves her from wasting time trying to do everything exactly right (*Fair,* 164).

After Ivy marries Oakley Fox and moves back up to the family farm at Sugar Fork, she bears twin sons, Bill and Danny Ray (born on Christmas Eve, 1929), and daughters LuIda (1935) and Maudy (1936). Apparently Joli was born in 1918. Now she feels the drain of mothering, for that is also a truth of mothering, as Smith reminds us:

> Silvaney, I have been caught up for so long in a great soft darkness, a blackness so deep and so soft that you can fall in there and get comfortable and never know you are falling in at all, and never land, just keep on falling. I wonder now if this is what happened to Momma. . . . I am so tired. . . . Maudy is the prettiest little baby I have ever had, but when she sucks it is like she is sucking the life right out of me. (*Fair,* 195)

She is 37 when she writes this; she will not feel alive again for three more years, not until Honey Breeding, the erotic who makes her alive again: "It is like I've had an electric shock. So now I am so much alive, I am tingling. I believe I know how you felt, Silvaney. For the first time, I know. I am on fire. I can feel it running through my veins and out my fingers" (*Fair,* 210).

Ivy's venture into the wild, from its beginning in the spring-house, restores her joy in the world: "And I love it here! Honey-suckle vines have grown up all over the bushes along the path, and wild white roses all down the steps. . . . It is like another world" (*Fair,* 213). What Honey Breeding does is make Ivy recognize that she is a queen: "Then he grabbled . . . down in the bag . . . and came up with the Queen" (*Fair,* 215). Then he makes Ivy a crown of starflowers. When she protests that she is too old to be a princess, he says "then you look like a Queen" (*Fair,* 230). But what of her relationship with her family?

> And yet you know that I love Oakley. He is my life. I love this farm, and these children, and Oakley, with all my heart. But there is something about a man that is *too good* which will drive you crazy. . . . It makes you want to dance in the thunderstorm. . . . For a long time I thought I was old. . . .
>   But now I am on fire. (*Fair,* 210)

Ivy's erotic love for Honey Breeding enables her to return to the farm, the family, and the children and love them with all her heart, for her heart is then larger. That is precisely what that great, ecstatic, imaginative love does, according to Smith:

> You know Silvaney, it is a funny thing, but that time I ran off with Honey Breeding helped not hurt, with me and Oakley. He has been *new* for me ever since, some way, and me for him, and even though I am way too old now to think on such things, I blush to say they come to mind often, they do! I am always ready for Oakley to lay me down. Back when I was lost in darkness, it was not so. For when you are caught so far down, you can not imagine the sun, or see a ray of sunshine any place. (*Fair,* 269-70)

Honey Breeding and Ivy are light. Her capacity for mothering has broadened, as has her need for selfhood. Ivy mothers children other than her own in the course of the novel. She takes in Violet Gay-heart's retarded daughter, Martha, and Joli's son, David, after Joli's divorce. But in her old age, more than anything else, she wants to be alone. Ivy is a mother, but she is not defined by motherhood.

Conclusion

In her essay "From Shadow to Substance: The Empowerment of the Artist Figure in Lee Smith's Fiction," Katherine Kearns traces throughout Smith's fiction the ambivalence about the dual roles of artist and mother. Ivy's demurral that "I never became a writer atall. Instead I have loved, and loved, and loved" (*Fair*, 315) testifies to the conflict but suggests a solution, for Ivy is a writer. Roz Kaveney, reviewing *Oral History, Family Linen,* and *Fair and Tender Ladies,* also points to the solution: "If Lee Smith has a weakness as a writer, it is that she writes at her best when she writes out of love" (Kaveney, 803). If Smith writes at her best when she writes out of love, then the writing and the love nourish each other. As with maternal-motherliness and sex-sensuousness, the disjunction between maternal-motherliness and art-artist is false.

Not only is Smith's reconciliation of male-female rich, vast, and broad in *Fair and Tender Ladies,* but so is her reconciliation of female-female rich, vast, and broad. One of the most interesting things to trace in Smith's fiction is the development of this character who is Brooke, Lily, Crystal, Dory, Pearl, and then Fay, and who finally reaches a kind of culmination in Silvaney, or rather in Ivy's preservation of Silvaney. In her various guises she is an essential part of the female psyche. First self-consciously shallowed, then catatonic, then irreparably – by biology and society – maimed, this female core in Silvaney is again irreparably maimed, but she is saved through a woman's remembrance, through female honoring of the female. In Silvaney this female core is finally internalized.

Ivy burns the letters to Silvaney at the end of the novel, saying that the letters did not matter, "it was the writing of them that signified" (*Fair*, 313). The connection between Ivy and Silvaney is mutually redemptive. Each saves, preserves, and allows for the existence of the other and for "female creativity as a necessary and sufficient condition" (Friedrich, 117).

In fact, the epigraph to *Fair and Tender Ladies* alerts us to this necessary and sufficient condition. It validates a woman's life and strength. It validates the woman-woman connection and women's stories. It promises hope in "Fill my cup." It even valorizes women's grief, and their ability to withstand it by sharing it. And they will not stop,

no, not for God Himself, not even if he rode
astride a fine white horse and bore the Crown
of Glory in his hands.[7]

Chapter Eight

Lee Smith in Context

Lee Smith is an important writer. She is trying to teach us, and herself, the value of the devalued, trivialized female way and that female selves cannot be whole until they recognize that value. Part of that recognition demands that they use their imaginations and the written word to find more constructive roles in society.[1] Her fiction explores how females are damaged, with a concomitant loss of soul. This exploration links to a felt loss of soul in Western culture that is linked elsewhere to damage of females.[2] Furthermore, Smith explores in her fiction how authentic male-female connection cannot exist without mutual recognition of the value of what we call feminine – in fact, mutual recognition of the value of both male and female principles, with no destructive compulsion to valorize one over the other, but rather to experience both, which is possible only through authentic link with the Other.

Smith's fiction is about the sacralizing of the female and of female sexuality, seeing female flesh as sacred as male flesh. Her characters need to be directly expressive and aggressive about their sexuality without being labeled nymphomaniacs, as the *Oxford Companion to American Literature* labels William Faulkner's Caddy and Quentin. Her fiction searches for the intersection between sex and sanctity and the intersection between wildness and domesticity. She is interested in the authentic female self and the authentic artistic self, which in her fiction are found in authentic relationship and authentic language. Her fiction searches for a language of the heart, and for real images of what one can be. Imagination is the key.

Because she is so at the heart of cultural imaginings, Lee Smith has been a national presence almost from the beginning of her career. That presence has been secured with the commercial and critical successes of the novels since *Black Mountain Breakdown*. Certainly since *Oral History* she has been an international presence.

Arguably, she has been that, too, from the time her first novel, *The Last Day the Dogbushes Bloomed*, was translated into German. But what is inarguable is that *Oral History*, *Family Linen*, and *Fair and Tender Ladies* have established Smith as an important contemporary writer capable of growth and development. The *New York Times* judged *Fair and Tender Ladies* Smith's "most ambitious and most fully realized novel to date" (Kinsella, 9). She has also been established firmly as a southern writer, holding her own when measured against the standards for comparison. Like Faulkner, she seems to have claimed as her own a small territory in the American landscape, as well as in the imagination. Frances Taliaferro, reviewing *Oral History* in *Harper's*, characterized the novel as "a portrait of a corner of America that I'm coming to think of as Lee Smith country" (Taliaferro, 74).

In assessing or analyzing Lee Smith's work, at least in the national press, the names of Eudora Welty, Flannery O'Connor, Carson McCullers, and William Faulkner are often, if not usually, invoked. Smith does not object to being categorized as a southern writer: "I think there are people who resist being called southern writers because they find it is in some way limiting or derogatory – or woman writer, or Appalachian writer. All those labels are applied to me, and they apply to me. I think you have to write out of your own experience, or it is truly not valid" (Hill, 16). She goes on to characterize part of the inheritance of the southern writer as "the givens of the southern experience – the concern with the past, the interest in religion, the importance of the family" (Hill, 17). But like any writer, Smith takes the givens and conventions of southern literature and the southern experience and filters them through the prism of her own experience, and something new is born. Collapsing her into Welty, O'Connor, McCullers, and Faulkner is an oversimplification, a tendency to see all the South and all southern literature as a single stereotype.

Lee Smith and the Past

The Myth of Aphrodite

Lee Smith is in a liminal position both as a woman and as a native of a region – the remote reaches of the southern Appalachian mountains—that lies outside the cultural mainstream. Her fiction is about the liminality of women and demonstrates how the female imagination can question existing cultural constructs and seek new syntheses. All Smith's early work is preoccupied with failed development of women, none of whom is able to locate a self that is authentic and can be fully expressed in society. Her early novels find every socially available path to development for her female characters leading to the inevitable psychic paralysis of Crystal Spangler in *Black Mountain Breakdown*. The crisis is profound, and it is a crisis at once spiritual, societal, and psychological. Most deeply, the crisis is sexual.

The female characters who suffer most are the sparkling, shimmering ones, suffused with sexuality and sensuality that can find no permissible expression, charged with energy that can find no outlet. Crystal Spangler's name alludes to that shimmering quality and also points to the problem: "In many dreams the nuclear center, the Self . . . appears as a crystal. The mathematically precise arrangement of a crystal evokes in us the intuitive feeling that even in so-called 'dead' matter, there is a spiritual ordering principle at work. Thus the crystal often symbolically stands for the union of extreme opposites—of matter and spirit" (von Franz, 221).

The paralyzing of Crystal's potential, then, springs from her failure to achieve the synthesis her name suggests as possible. She colludes—via her passivity—with the dualism in the cultural idiom that splits spirit and matter. The consequence of this dualism, as embedded in our religious constructs, has led to the devaluation of matter and consequent devaluation of nature and thus of women, who are linked to nature.[3]

Cultural taboos against sexuality in general and against active females specifically—against sexually active adult females—are responsible for the suffering of women such as Crystal. Smith's imagination finds a solution by resurrecting the sacred, sexually active adult female. This part of female psychology was variously imaged as Sumerian Inanna, Semitic Ishtar(s), Phoenician Astarte, Canaanite Anat, Sidonian Astarte or Asherah, Egyptian Hathor or Isis, Cybele of ancient Asia Minor, Old Irish Morrigan, Greek Aphrodite, and Roman Venus, among others, in cultures that worshiped her. The dawn goddesses—Vedic Ushas, Greek Eos, Roman Aurora, and the proto-Baltic Sun Maiden—should be included for their activeness and ability to

stir all creatures to motion, and for other characteristics that link
them to the sex and war goddesses as well. Smith's red and gold
imagery links her characters both to the sun goddesses and the sex
and war goddesses.

Smith's fictive search leads to many characteristics most fully expressed in the classical Greek Aphrodite. In *The Meaning of
Aphrodite*, Paul Friedrich traces the "naked goddess we have known
since the beginning of time" through her various incarnations as
Inanna, Ishtar, Astarte, Aphrodite, Venus, and the Old Irish
Morrigan. Friedrich says Aphrodite's sexuality adds another dimension of liminality, that of the active female. Smile-loving or penis-
loving, variant translations for Aphrodite's common epithet Philom-
meides (Friedrich, 202-204), Aphrodite goes outward actively, like
her prototype Inanna, whose eye ointment is called "Let him come,
Let him come" and whose breastplate is called "Come, man, come!"[4]
The classical Aphrodite "presents an image of relative sexual equality
and an active female role that dynamically contradicts the sexual
double standard of the early texts. In a male-dominated culture like
that reflected in Homer and Hesiod, even a relatively active woman
defies and threatens and crosses over fundamental categories"
(Friedrich, 141). Aphrodite "asserts or even demands a crossing-over
between emotional antitheses or a simultaneous affirmation of them"
(Friedrich, 7).

The impulse of Western literature has often been marked by the
attempt to restore sanctity to the culturally degraded human experience of sexuality, the quality the Provençal poets called *quel remir*
("sexual radiance"). Sexual vitality can be seen bursting in the skins
of Smith's golden women like Sharon DuBois ("of the woods") in
Fancy Strut: "Something was alive and jumping inside Sharon, something that was always on the verge of breaking the skin to escape. It
was exciting" (*Strut*, 50). But these female characters live in small
southern towns locked in a rigid traditional culture that forbids direct expression of female sexuality, so that it gets perverted in various ways.

Friedrich explores how the avoidance of Aphrodite in Western
cultural tradition points to pathology in the development of the
Western definition of the feminine. He demonstrates that the standard works have either belittled or left out altogether this powerful
figure who constitutes the image of human sexual love as sacred.

Books by specialists on Greek myth or religion "typically allot only a few words or phrases to her, and these are often disparaging ones" (Friedrich, 1). He identifies "nonavoiders" such as Walter Otto (1954), Marcel Detienne (1972), and Charles Seltman (1956), and Seltman he quotes as having put the issue very well: " 'Of all the Twelve Olympians she is the most alarming and the most alluring, so much so that many writers have tended to edge away from a discussion of her. It is not that they write against Aphrodite, but rather that they avoid her as a topic' " (Friedrich, 1).

In *Oral History*, whose title suggests a reconciliation of opposites, Smith discovers what has been lost: a goddess. With the loss of the goddess, mythic roles for women were lost. We can identify the figures of Red Emmy and Dory as Friedrich's goddess, whose power generates from their embodying the sacred image who is, in fact, the conjugation of sex and religion. When Smith delves into the mountains, her native southern Appalachians, and plumbs the oral culture for something living from the past, what she finds – although I am quite sure this is largely unconscious – is Aphrodite. The message is so radical that she obscures the latent content, probably even from herself, with the manifest content.

Seeking a vision of wholeness in adulthood, Smith finds with *Oral History* a place and time where spirit and flesh, mind and world, and language and thought are not divided, and where domesticity includes wildness and passion. She hears the ancient mountain song and lets the healing images emerge, from her own unconscious and from the mythic past, and "the music that breathes" is Aphrodite (Friedrich, 220).

The outburst of *Oral History*, clearly so much richer than anything Smith had written up to that point, seems to find at least a partial solution to the arrest of the female psyche. The nature of that solution places Smith firmly in the current reexamination of the Western tradition. Like psychologist Carol Gilligan and theologian Carol Christ, Smith is looking for a mythology that permits female development and permits female embodiment of the sacred. *Oral History* retraces the history of the species and seeks what is missing, what has been left out, in the way the Western tradition has chosen to tell that history. With relocation in space and time, in the lore-steeped Appalachian mountains and in the mythic past, Smith's imagination shakes free to burst the bonds of history and find the

missing goddess who bridges the traditional oppositions of sex and
purity, nature and culture.

Eudora Welty

Although Smith recognized her own material when, as a student at
Hollins, she read Eudora Welty, she is doing something very different
with that material. Welty is concerned with specific communities in
the Old South and the rhythm of daily life. Smith's concern is with
the female psyche, and partly her fictional interest lies with its dislocation in the New South. Welty gives the reader snapshot truths of
times and places. Smith's concerns are both broader and narrower.
Whereas Welty finds the universal in the microcosm, Smith is looking
for what specifically belongs to the feminine while she questions, in
a way Welty does not, cultural definitions of what constitutes the
universal. This questioning in some ways makes Smith's fiction more
uncomfortable, more deeply disquieting, than Welty's. It is also more
uneven, for it seeks to critique and go beyond the given context, not
simply to portray it. Furthermore, the New South in which Smith's
community of characters pitches its tent is more diffuse than is possible in Welty's Mississippi. But Smith's deepest concern is with the
female psyche and its potential for expansion, with the flow and ebb
of the psyche, not with the flow and ebb of daily life. Smith's effec-
tiveness as a writer in part stems from her portrayal of the psychic
dislocation of southern women in times of rapid cultural change
(Jennings, 10).

Still, Smith rightly recognized her own material – and her own
self – in reading and hearing the work of Eudora Welty. After all,
Smith is a southern woman, dealing with southern settings and
southern talk – her characters sometimes are found in classic Welty
locales, in beauty shops and corner markets – but her concerns are
different. Welty is interested in female characters, but Smith's interest
is the female imagination. Smith is vitally interested in female roles in
the community and how women do and do not fit into the community, and she deeply explores ways women are damaged by the cir-
cumscriptions of society and community, especially southern. In her
first books that damage was all she was interested in, because she
was scared that there were no other possibilities for women.

Damaged females populate all of Smith's fiction, from Brooke to
Monica to Crystal to Dory to Faye to Silvaney. In the novels following

Black Mountain Breakdown Smith began to find ennobling images for women. At first her female characters are just damaged, as Smith explored the prescribed, community-validated paths to identity for women and found them all ending at the ledge of the suicide leap. Smith was exploring whether women could be fully realized and accepted for their essential selves within communities, but seemed to find that they could not, and what is more, that they colluded in their own corruption, destruction, and erasure. Writing about something new in what both writer and reader sense is a different era from Welty's, with different concerns for women, Smith explores what Judith Thurman found missing in Margaret Atwood's fiction: the intellectual courage to write about "a woman's complicity in her sexual corruption; about her feelings of emptiness and delight in power; about her lust, anger, and impotence; about her yearning for trust and despair of wholeness."[5] Through the power of the written word, Smith begins to imagine a conclusion beyond complicity and destruction. Her fiction is redemptive, finally, because wholeness, not damage, is what Smith is seeking.

Flannery O'Connor

Like Flannery O'Connor, Smith is interested in – in fact, consumed by – wholeness. The impulse of the work of both writers is to restore human wholeness denied by the rational, the scientific, the materialistic, the moralistic, the pornographic modern mind. Both writers are concerned with embodiment. O'Connor's pervasive theme is that the spirit is expressed through the flesh; it either dwells in the flesh or does not live. O'Connor, who will always be considered a Catholic writer, was a devout Catholic who nevertheless drove again and again toward the failure of the Catholic faith to sustain its own avowed belief that flesh is spirit-filled. O'Connor is trying to demonstrate a truth of her Catholic creed, although a creed often obscured by leaders of her faith – that spirit is here in the flesh and operates through the flesh. Her work is an accusation against Christians who succumb to the mind-body dichotomy that has been part of Western thought at least since decadent late-Greek thought (coincident temporally with the historical Jesus) inserted into Christianity by Paul. (Smith's short story "St. Paul" recognizes the turn to transcendence as the partner of materialism – just as Griffin's study *Pornography and Silence* recognizes the doctrinal mind as the twin

of the pornographic mind – and shows how both erase female flesh.)
O'Connor shocks us intentionally because she presumes we are ma-
terialists and do not believe it. And yet despite repeated intellectual
efforts to move beyond dualism – Alfred North Whitehead characterized the mind-body dichotomy as "quite unbelievable"[6] – we have
been unable to do so.

Smith, unlike O'Connor, is not working from the certainty of any
creed. She is more modern than O'Connor; she cannot start from
that creed because, in her universe, that faith is outworn. Smith explores religion as one avenue for wholeness, but the religion available to her characters is so corrupted that it offers nothing but hol-
lowness and cynicism. In O'Connor, too, institutionalized religion is
usually corrupted and debased, but she has misfits who are truly inspired, who shine as saints against her pragmatic, bourgeois characters impatient with the radical claims of religion. Like Smith,
O'Connor mistrusts the cult of progress. But, unlike Smith, she believes that the church is the channel of grace in the world and is
necessary, even when it is corrupted. Smith is searching for the spirit
in the flesh, but she has to imagine it, without the help of any dogma.
Furthermore, surrounded by cultural images produced by the twin
pornographic and doctrinal attitudes that deny it, Smith is searching
for the spirit in *female* flesh. That attempt, that effort of imagination,
is arguably the central impetus of her fiction. She is trying to imagine
the flesh as inspired, as filled with spirit, as alive because of spirit,
and as dead if spirit is locked out by the conventions of scientific rationalism and rigid social codes that disallow or deny female spiritu-
ality, vitality, creativity, originality, expression, sexuality.

Carson McCullers

Smith does not validate the loner-misfit of McCullers at all. In fact,
she is vehemently opposed to any romanticization of that stance. If
there is any hope for them at all, her characters have to become self-
realized through connection and relation. McCullers's characters are
damaged and dismissed by mainstream society, and they live out
tragic lives of alienation, thereby achieving a hint of moral elevation.
If anything, Smith exposes such characters as sick and fraudulent.
She does have quirky characters, but she is looking for wholeness in
the norm, not in the misfit. She may imagine the misfit to try to
imagine what modern society has left out, but her misfits show dam-

age to the self. Smith is trying to recoup those lost parts of ourselves that the patriarchal, the rational, the scientific – and, for her characters, the trendy – deny.

William Faulkner

It is Faulkner who can most correctly be called Smith's southern progenitor. All her females may be seen as Caddy's daughters. *The Sound and the Fury* is about the warping of Caddy's great capacity for love. Crystal, Dory, Pearl, Faye, and Silvaney are all daughters of Caddy – infinitely beautiful, infinitely damaged, and warped in their great capacity for love.

In *Absalom, Absalom!* (a novel about the horror latent in patriarchal legacy) Faulkner tried to write about Caddy Compson and Judith Sutpen as women of action with the capacity to love. But he could not really imagine them, so he could not really write about them past childhood. Both characters' womanhood is blighted precisely because of their gifts. Their courage seems to have damned them. This twist is both ironic and tragic, because in Faulkner the few characters who are able to love are those who are not afraid to fight. Judith Sutpen, her eyes shining as she hides in the loft watching her father stripped naked to the waist wrestling with slaves, puts her cowardly brother to shame; Caddy Compson, climbing the pear tree in her muddy drawers to peer in the window at Damuddy's funeral, is braver than any of her brothers on the ground. It was this image – a girl braver than any of her brothers – that Faulkner says made him fall in love with Caddy. With both Judith and Caddy, he worshiped their possibilities when young – their sharpness, perceptiveness, honesty, and courage; their restless questioning, their refusal to just accept.

David Williams says that Caddy stands for "underlying mind function, movement that will not be halted" (7) – in other words, the active female, Aphrodite. But either Faulkner's personal limitations or those imposed by the culture prevented his being able to imagine how such women could function in society, so they were doomed. He fell in love with Caddy, his heart's darling, but because she was an ideal he could not fully imagine, he silenced her forever. Like the early Smith, Faulkner could not imagine how the creative, brilliant, and sensual female could be accommodated by a society that was

built on negation of her. So, like the early Smith, he could not imagine an alternative for her.

As Richard Burlage did Dory, Faulkner left the sensual female
fallen and silenced forever by this world and himself. Faulkner could
easily imagine how a Caroline Compson could function: he imaged
with brutal clarity the tyranny of weakness, wielding its tools of manipulation and martyrdom. But Caddy – the bright, creative, wild
child, his love – was lost, glimpsed in a Nazi staff car as an adult and
imagined to be the mistress of a high-ranking Nazi, the prisoner-play-
thing of the male principle at its most unyielding. Faulkner saw too
clearly what was all around him, as well as what was coming. But
Smith saw another, more distant, but not impossible truth – that
Caddy could be picked up, if women would do so, and go on. Smith
gave her daughters, and daughters' daughters, and they slowly began
to vanquish the structures that Faulkner so rightly saw.

Faulkner is in some ways Smith's progenitor, but only in part.
Smith is not male, is not a mannered aristocrat, and is not writing
with a code in mind. Smith encounters and resists that South head-
on (and was apparently horrified at the exercise of privilege she saw)
at St. Catherine's. But Smith is a firmly grounded woman from the
Appalachian region, and the dialectic of her work lies first between
the aristocratic South and her mountain origins, but it then goes beyond to develop through creative imagination its own frontier.
Smith's writing is southern, but not simply southern. After all, America's greatest literature of a type has always come from some particular region's speaking about things that lie far beyond. Welty and
Faulkner have not only entered but *are* the American mainstream.
Equally, if not more so, the writing of Lee Smith brings the regional
into the world domain as she deals with the problems of the female
and her imagination in an age of radical transition, problems faced
with pain and poignancy by most of the world's females.

An additional, and not unrelated, point of distinction is that
Faulkner is obsessed with the mother-son relationship. He blames
many of the problems of obsessive males – their overriding concern
with eternity and their inability to live in this world – on their having
been inadequately mothered. The mother images in Faulkner's fiction are terrible. Smith is on to something different. Many of her
mother images are lovely, but she gives women other noble images,
beyond the admirable one of mother. Many of her most successful

women are not much mothered; they seem to thrive with autonomy and free range of course, that may be explained by her gravitation toward the Aphrodite complex). Furthermore, Smith can do what Faulkner cannot. It takes her a while, but she does learn to imagine these women – the women with beauty, intellect, and capacity for public action and expression and the capacity to love – as successful adults. She can imagine them as daughters of Dilsey as well as daughters of Caddy, able to survive in the day-to-day and to see and accept life's cycles. That is not to say that she capitulates to a male code for such characters. These women do not retreat to a masculine perspective, always bought at the price of distance. Rather, Smith reimagines what successful might mean for such a woman, full of life and ability to love. She partly imagines it by allowing domesticity and wildness to coexist in one female body, and she tries to imagine such a liberating coexistence for men as well. Smith succeeds, and this is a victory for us all.

Smith's Influence on Others

Renewal for culture, one of the functions of literature, often seems to come from the border – the edge, the fringe, the marginalized, however that is imagined or constituted. The South has become Americanized, homogenized, and, especially, urbanized in many ways. Yet the so-called border states, which are strung between the South and the North along the southern Appalachian mountains and beyond, are still a marginalized world, unlike the urban South. From three of these border states – from the Appalachian coal mining region of Virginia and West Virginia and from the farmland of western Kentucky – have come the remarkable fiction of Lee Smith, Bobbie Ann Mason, and Jayne Anne Phillips.

Although Mason sounds like Smith, it is Phillips who truly is like Smith. Mason and Smith share an infallible ear for southern dialect and its humor, a sense of its truth in stories, a love for it as home. But Smith and Phillips come from the same corner. It is a part of the country that has seen structures deteriorate on ruined land – abandoned mines and slag heaps litter their fiction – and where there is an overwhelming elegiac sense, which they share. Somehow they developed the same concern with the female psyche, the same urge to explore female identity, the same attempt to imagine the future. Smith shares her ear, her humor, and her whimsy with Mason, but she shares her urgency for the need of Eros, her intuitive grasp of the female psyche, and her deepest concerns with Phillips.

Bobbie Ann Mason

Mason recognized her material in Smith, just as Smith recognized hers in Welty. But although the surface humor and setting of their fictions may look the same, although their characters may often be from the same social world, the concerns of their fictions are different. Mason's concerns are social, not psychological. She does not share with Smith the concern with female psyche and identity. If anything, Mason is more concerned about the effects of social change on men – one reason she has been taken so quickly into the mainstream. She is a social observer, and she is politically astute. She is imagining new family structures and a new social consciousness, using the 1960s as a touchstone. She has much to offer from her observation, but it is not the same as Smith's offering. Their fictions are doing entirely different things. Mason is trying to reclaim the lives of her characters from snobbish derogation, from being trivialized and marginalized. Her people want in; they want to be part of mainstream American culture and to share in its rewards.

Mason's sensibility is antisnobbery; she believes we are overly concerned with being civilized. She allows her people to have insights into their lives, and in this way has brought them at least into the mainstream of American fiction, if not of American culture. Smith is working on something different. She is showing how stereotypes really do limit people's lives, how failure of imagination causes people to lapse into prescribed images. Her characters do not have insights because of the way that society's images constrain and define their lives, stifling the imagination and self-expression that would have saved them.

Jayne Anne Phillips

Underneath the surface it is Jayne Anne Phillips who is swimming the same deep stream with Smith. Phillips's fiction does not look like Smith's on the surface. Phillips does not use dialect; in some ways her characters could be from anywhere, and she does not use quirky mannerisms to identify those characters as southern. But Phillips is dealing with the wounded female psyche and the business of self-repair just as surely as Smith is. They are both looking for wholeness, really, and for new images.

The similarities in their sensibilities may spring from their shared origins in the Appalachian coal-mining regions, a part of the country where the demands of a technological nation have taken a visible toll on natural beauty. Here the earth is littered with the ruins of progress, where the cost of ideas of glory is tallied in piercing visual reminders: falling-down and abandoned structures, raped and ravaged earth, broken lives. Ruined and abandoned beauty is the silent message of the landscape, as the mostly impoverished indigents are left to ponder the mutilation of great forests, the scars of strip-mining, the degradation of a people and their language.

If females are equated with nature and males with culture, as has been argued by scholars, then the observation of the waste of beauty in the Appalachian coal-mining regions must have been instructive and perhaps more than a little chilling for Smith and Phillips, who spent the long days and nights of girlhood contemplating it. But by the same token, Smith and Phillips had in their origins access to other myths – mountain myths that go back through Celtic song and story to earlier mythologies that included goddesses and a sense of nature as sacred. Whereas much of Phillips's *Black Tickets* was thin or read like a writing exercise, her completely successful *Machine Dreams*, a semiautobiographical novel, is suffused with mythic elements. And as for Smith, she was unable to imagine a mythic role for women until she turned back to mountain songs, mountain culture, and mountain women. Her healing seems almost to have begun with Red Emmy and her storyteller, Granny Younger, the chthonian healer of *Oral History* who knows herbs and mountain lore and participates fully in the life of the community. Mystery for Smith's fictive moderns has become so banal that it is unlikely to turn up anywhere except in the *National Enquirer*, while Phillips says that what she is writing about is the deracination of her generation. Both portray, in their fiction, the horror of isolation and the psychic wounding.

In Smith's Appalachians and in Phillips's West Virginia remain at least a memory of community and vestiges of parts of culture that have disappeared in mainstream American development. Mountain culture is not part of the scientific-rational-industrial culture, so it might have been possible for a woman to imagine playing a role like being a doctor, as Smith does with Granny Younger. Furthermore, mountain culture is marginal, not part of the mainstream economic world, so that notions of respectability have not yet put the death grip on everything impulsive, erotic, or original in life. Smith and Phillips are able to tap into something different. Having had that experience and then emerging into this world seems to have pushed their intellects to ask some probing questions.

Both are interested in how expression operates, how it either develops or stunts the self. False language falsifies the world, relationships, reality. False images also falsify the world. Phillips says that part of what her fiction is about is the tragedy of traditional male and female roles-stereotypes when those roles-stereotypes are no longer operable in society. She and Smith share a sense of horror and tragedy at the failure of authentic male-female connection. They also share a horror of what happens when either males or females desex themselves. Women in their fiction who act like men in order to operate efficiently in the world collude in hatred of the feminine way. The damage done by women to women, especially in Smith, is deeply explored. Sometimes this extends to the mother-daughter connection, important to both writers and often portrayed with profound tenderness, but its dark side is also presented. Danner, in an outtake of *Machine Dreams* later published as the short story "Blue Moon," is afraid that she is "in training to become my mother, become that kind of supremely competent, unfulfilled woman, vigilant and damaged,"[7] and Smith's managerial women do irreparable harm to the families they try to run like businesses.

Phillips and Smith share an intuitive grasp of the female psyche and the damage done by fear of or neglect by men, but they also share a longing to find the male – the missing or damaged brother, the formidable or inaccessible father. This longing they share with Mason, but for Mason it seems to be easier to imagine a male self, or to link to maleness. Both Phillips and Smith seek to restore the male to the female, to restore eros to the world. Brooke and Bentley and Crystal and Mack prefigure Danner and Billy, who in the mythic substratum of *Machine Dreams* are revealed to be the twins, brother and sister, of cosmic myth who can start the destroyed world over again.

African American Women Writers

In the unraveling of the patriarchy, Smith's work has been compared to that of African American women writers, especially Alice Walker and Toni Morrison. Like Walker, Smith's fiction searches for new definitions of the sacred. *The Temple of My Familiar* is perhaps the work closest in spirit and essence to *Oral History* in its search for the goddess and for new relationships between men and women. Both Smith and Walker have protagonists who cease praying to a male-imaged god outside of nature and begin praying to presences within nature. Both see the sacred-sexual as the new locus for what we call god.

Like Morrison, Smith "nibble[s] at the limits of empiricism" and does not demystify the irrational in her texts. "The possibilities raised in [*The Last Day the Dogbushes Bloomed*] informs Smith's later fiction. She continues to nibble at the limits of empiricism, offering, like Toni Morrison and Gabriel García Márquez, instances of magic in the realistic novel, and like them locating the magic within the roots of an oral culture" (Jones 1984, 256). All three are involved in a profound process of reimagining and renaming.

Like Smith, Morrison has male and female characters who are the same size – Pilate and Macon, Hagar and Milkman in *Song of Solomon*. And *Song of Solomon* has a sacrificial return to the earth, the bones of Macon and Pilate's father, which sets spirits free, as Ora Mae's return of the earrings to the earth in *Oral History* sets spirits free.

Morrison and Walker, as well as Smith, attempt to restore to its place of importance sweetness, which has been marginalized or ephemeralized by a male intellectual system that links the trait to stupidity or gullibility. In Morrison's character Sweet in *The Song of Solomon*, Walker's Shug (a southern term of endearment, short for *sugar*) of both *The Color Purple* and *The Temple of My Familiar*, and Smith's Candy of *Family Linen* and Honey of *Fair and Tender Ladies*, sweetness is shown as strength, and as necessary. Morrison's switching of the name Sugarman for Solomon – "the wise" – in the sacred song of *Song of Solomon* is another attempt to bridge characteristics, healing the false split between sweetness and wisdom. Blocked characters in the works of both novelists, like Guitar in *The Song of Solomon* and Ora Mae in *Oral History*, have trouble accepting or believing in sweetness; this failure blights their lives.

Validating Female Experience

Lee Smith cannot be called a doctrinaire feminist. She is neither political by nature nor polemical by intellectual predisposition. She
cannot bring herself to write in the omniscient voice, because she
wishes to be closer to her characters. This does not mean, however,
that she should be ignored by those interested in the female experience, which she explores with remarkable insight. Her truths are
told in stories, and they link to human experience rather than abstract thought. What she does fight for, however, is creative space,
room to explore, and sanction to grow past images into human
wholeness. She validates traditional female experience while questioning it and demanding more expansive alternatives. If she has any
agenda, it is that only through imagination can human beings be
linked to the world without being trapped by it. Perhaps her work is
radically feminist – its repudiation of loveless marriages, its insistence
on erotic connection, its evocation of the mother-daughter bond, its
assertion of nature over culture (evidenced in names of characters),
and, finally, its refusal to accept religious formulae that damn female
sensuality and female sensibility.

Into the world's record Lee Smith has, without apology, entered
a part of the female experience as a plea for human wholeness. The
end of *Fair and Tender Ladies* sets up the feminine body as a worthy entity. After all, women have been modeling themselves after
kings, heroes, and "man" (as in "if man is to survive") forever. Why
not posit "queens" as a worthy category for all human beings? There
are no bodies that are not sexed, and surely male-sexed bodies are
not the only bodies that can be set forth as universal categories.
What Lee Smith's writing does at its best is help all of us – as what we
are and what we can be – walk in our bodies like queens.

Notes and References

Introduction

1. Paul Friedrich, *The Meaning of Aphrodite* (Chicago: University of Chicago Press, 1978); hereafter cited in text.

2. Virginia A. Smith, "On Regionalism, Women's Writing, and Writing as a Woman: A Conversation with Lee Smith," *Southern Review* 26, no. 4 (Autumn 1990): 784-95; hereafter cited in text.

3. Ben Jennings, "Language and Reality in Lee Smith's *Oral History*," *Iron Mountain Review* 3, no. 1 (Winter 1986): 10; hereafter cited in text.

4. Jan Hoffert, "Writers' Renaissance in North Carolina," *Library Journal*, 1 November 1989, 48; hereafter cited in text.

5. Thulani Davis, "Southern Women Stake Their Claim," *Voice Literary Supplement*, February 1986, 11; hereafter cited in text.

6. *Newsweek*, 31 October 1988, 72H; hereafter cited in text.

7. *Liminal* is from *limen*, which is Latin for "threshold." The concepts of liminal and interstitial are central to Paul Friedrich's analysis of the meaning of Aphrodite and to this study. To be in a liminal position is to operate in the interstices between structures. In liminal positions are found the wellsprings of emotion. According to Friedrich,

> The liminal figures and images of myth often deny or contradict or challenge the basic categories of society and the ethical norms of a culture. A summary idea of the scope of the liminal may be had from the following set of contrasts or antitheses, which I find suggestive, although, as I fully realize, they raise many new questions. Thus, liminality often entails the following: 1. Transition or "crossover" between grids, structures, etc. 2. A bridging or vaulting over, or simply operating between, such cultural (and universal?) oppositions as nature/culture, good/evil, and beauty/ugliness 3. Asceticism *or* strong sexuality 4. Extreme verbal purity *or* excessive profanity and obscenity 5. Silence *or* verbal efflorescence and brilliance 6. Foolishness and silliness *or* great wisdom, seercraft, prescience 7. Social homogeneity *or* simply absence of relative status 8. Nakedness *or* special costumes. (133)

8. I believe this cross-disciplinary approach is not only fertile but mandatory for the things humanity is trying to understand.

Chapter One

1. Second Annual Writers' Conference, Virginia Commonwealth University, Richmond, 14 July 1989; hereafter cited in text as "Richmond, 1989."

2. Personal communication, Richmond, July 1989; hereafter cited in text as "pers. comm., 1989."

3. "Tongues of Fire," in *Me and My Baby View the Eclipse* (New York: G. P. Putnam's Sons, 1990), 111. Stories from this collection are hereafter cited in text as *Eclipse.*

4. Southern Arts Festival, University of North Carolina at Chapel Hill, April 1987; hereafter cited in text as "Chapel Hill, 1987."

5. Jonathan Yardley, "Bewitched Voices" (review of *Oral History*), *Washington Post*, 15 June 1983, B1; hereafter cited in text.

6. W. P. Kinsella, "Left behind on Blue Star Mountain" (review of *Fair and Tender Ladies*), *New York Times Book Review*, 18 September 1988, 9; hereafter cited in text.

7. *Fair and Tender Ladies* (New York: G. P. Putnam's Sons, 1988), 316; hereafter cited in text as *Fair.*

8. Dorothy Combs Hill, "An Interview with Lee Smith," *Southern Quarterly* 28, no. 2 (Winter 1990): 13; hereafter cited in text.

9. George Steiner, "Wording Our World," *New Yorker*, 19 June 1989, 98; hereafter cited in text.

10. Christopher Lehmann-Haupt, "Books of the Times" (review of *Oral History*), *New York Times*, 29 July 1983, C21; hereafter cited in text.

11. Doris Betts quoted in Lynn Jessup, *Greensboro News & Record*, 27 September 1987, H6; hereafter cited in text.

12. "Loose Characters" (review of Ellen Gilchrist's *Drunk with Love*), *Spectator*, 6-12 November 1986, 5; hereafter cited in text as "Loose."

13. Ken Ringle, "Lee Smith at Home with Her Muse," *Washington Post*, 4 December 1988, F5; hereafter cited in text.

14. Letter to the author, June 1987.

15. Katherine Kearns, "Lee Smith," *Dictionary of American Biography Yearbook: 1983* (Detroit: Gale Research, 1984), 316; hereafter cited in text as "Kearns 1984."

16. It is interesting that the first story in which Smith returns to her native mountains for setting, "Heat Lightning," is the only other place in her fiction besides "Tongues of Fire" where ecstatic utterance marks personal change, spiritual release. In some ways it seems to be release from conventional, white, overcivilized religion. This is clearer in "Tongues of Fire," but Geneva – the housewife of "Heat Lightning" who "feels a change coming on" and begins to "holler out" in church – imagines leaving the spiritual aridity of her marriage behind and running away with a carnival man

to wash her clothes "on every rock in every river in the world" (*Cakewalk* [New York: G. P. Putnam's Sons, 1981], 124, 134. Stories from this collection are hereafter cited in text as *Cakewalk*). The carnival man, whose voice is "different and strange," is "dark-faced with long curly hair like a gypsy and he has something in his hand" (*Cakewalk*, 132). What he has in his hand, which he gives to Geneva's son, is "a little green and red plastic snake with sequin eyes." When Geneva looks down "to get away from his eyes the skin on her legs looks so white" (*Cakewalk*, 132).

17. Smith discusses Tom Wolfe's *The New Journalism* and how she adapted the downstage narrator to solve "all the ambivalence" she feels toward her characters in "The Voice behind the Story," in *Voicelust: Eight Contemporary Fiction Writers on Style*, ed. Allen Wier and Don Hendrie, Jr. (Lincoln: University of Nebraska Press, 1985), 93-100; hereafter cited in text as "Voice."

18. "My editor at Harper & Row was this marvelous man, Cass Canfield Sr. A very remarkable individual – he went to Mexico and retrieved Trotsky's bloodstained manuscript; he went to Russia and smuggled out Solzhenitsyn's first manuscripts. But he didn't edit at all! Just took my books and published them. And no marketing whatsoever" (Robert Draper, *American Way*, 1 February 1989, n.p.).

19. Mark Scandling, "Staying in Touch with the Real World," *Carolina Quarterly* 32, no. 1 (Winter 1980): 54.

20. "Mrs. Darcy Meets the Blue-Eyed Stranger at the Beach" (*Carolina Quarterly* 30, no. 2 [Spring-Summer 1978]: 65-77) was published in *Prize Stories 1979: The O. Henry Awards*, ed. William Abrahams (New York: Doubleday, 1979), 227-41. "Between the Lines" (*Carolina Quarterly* 32, no. 1 [Winter 1980]: 42-51) was published in *Prize Stories 1981: The O. Henry Awards*, ed. William Abrahams (New York: Doubleday, 1981), 81-93.

21. Faith Sale, personal communication, July 1989.

22. Frederick Busch, "Voices of Hoot Owl Holler" (review of *Oral History*), *New York Times Book Review*, 10 July 1983, 15; hereafter cited in text.

23. Frances Taliaferro, review of *Oral History*, *Harper's*, July 1983, 74; hereafter cited in text.

24. *Oral History* (New York: G. P. Putnam's Sons, 1983); hereafter cited in text as *Oral*.

25. Hal Crowther, personal communication, July 1989.

26. Jan Hoffman, "Booker Creek Breakdown" (review of *Family Linen*), *Village Voice*, 15 October 1985, 56; hereafter cited in text.

27. Denise Giardina, "Beautiful, Awful, and Misunderstood," *Belles Lettres* 4, no. 3 (Spring 1989): 10; hereafter cited in text.

Chapter Two

1. In June 1990 George Franklin, the father of Susan's childhood friend, Eileen Franklin-Lipsher, was accused by the state of California of the rape and murder of Susan Nason on 22 September 1969 (see *Time*, 4 June 1990, 56).

2. The October 1991 debate that arose when law professor Anita Hill testified before the Senate Judiciary Committee that Supreme Court nominee Clarence Thomas had sexually harassed her demonstrated once again how the male, regardless of race, who allies himself with traditionally male institutions is invested with credibility. Polls demonstrated female collusion with the patriarchy. Mythological underpinnings were laid bare by references in the media to Professor Hill's "opening Pandora's box." Language used against Hill as she returned home demonstrated the persistence of cultural formulae manifested in the disposal of Susan Nason's body: airport hecklers called Hill "a piece of trash" (*Washington Post*, 20 October 1991, 1). The Charles Stuart case in Boston, however, demonstrated that the greatest capacity to be believed is the birthright, first and foremost, of the white male.

3. On this conflict in Smith's work, see Katherine Kearns, "From Shadow to Substance: The Empowerment of the Artist Figure in Lee Smith's Fiction," in *Writing the Woman Artist*, ed. Suzanne W. Jones (Philadelphia: University of Pennsylvania Press, 1991), 175-95; hereafter cited in text as "Kearns 1991."

4. Naming and renaming were crucial for identity and destiny in the ancient world. In the Judaic tradition Abram's name is changed to Abraham when god calls him to his destiny; Abraham means "father of many nations" (Genesis 17:5). After Jacob wrestles with the angel, his name is changed to Israel, "he who strives with god" – *isra*, "he who strives with," and *el*, "gog" (Genesis 32:28). *El* itself was the name of a foreign god that the Hebrews subsumed as one of the many names of their god. That name is echoed in *Oral History* with Eli, the name of Dory's brother. He has one of the names for god; she is missing the name for god (*Dory* is close to the more common *Dorothy* minus *theos*). Simon's name is changed to Peter, or "rock," when Christ says, "upon this rock I will build my church" (Matthew 17:18). I am grateful to Dr. Kenneth Craig for pointing out to me the biblical importance of renaming. Name changing was equally important in Celtic mythology.

5. *Black Mountain Breakdown* (New York: G. P. Putnam's Sons, 1980), 187; hereafter cited in text as *Black*.

Chapter Three

1. Joseph Campbell, *Historical Atlas of World Mythology*, vol. 1, *The Way of the Animal Powers*, part 1, "Mythologies of the Primitive Hunters

and Gatherers" (New York: Harper & Row, 1988), 9; hereafter cited in text as "Campbell 1988."

2. Quoted in Judith Thurman, "Choosing a Place" (review of Nadine Gordimer's *A Sport of Nature*), *New Yorker*, 29 June 1987, 88.

3. *The Last Day the Dogbushes Bloomed* (New York: Harper & Row, 1968), 171; hereafter cited in text as *Last*.

4. See M. E. Combs-Schilling, *Sacred Performances: Islam, Sexuality, and Sacrifice* (New York: Columbia University Press, 1989), 233-44 and especially 262-68; hereafter cited in text.

5. According to Patricia Monaghan, "The queen of heaven . . . may have been the life-giving sun itself" (*The Book of Goddesses and Heroines* [New York: Dutton, 1981], 150; hereafter cited in text). Note the reconciliation of opposites in "night sun."

6. David Williams, *Faulkner's Women* (Toronto: University of Toronto Press, 1980), 7; hereafter cited in text.

7. Leonard Rogoff, *Carolina Quarterly* 26, no. 1 (1974): 110-14.

8. See Thurman ("Choosing a Place") for a discussion of the evil of white-family-as-sanctuary, one of Nadine Gordimer's themes. Eugenia's first name suggests that Eugene is part of the creativity principle; both her first name and her last defy (or embrace) categories.

9. Alice Walker, *The Color Purple* (New York: Harcourt, 1982), 242; hereafter cited in text.

10. Toni Morrison has a significant image of a woman in a yellow dress in *Tar Baby*, and the color is also an indicator of Aphrodite.

11. Williams discusses this theme in Faulkner: "Woman is thus defeated and her order overturned, this time by a male principle of intellect devoted to finding a code of existence apart from the feminine element of blood" (Williams, 213).

12. Francine Prose, "Confident at 11, Confused at 16" (a report on the work of Carol Gilligan), *New York Times Magazine*, 7 January 1990, 23-46.

13. *Something in the Wind* (New York: Harper & Row, 1971), 15; hereafter cited in text as *Wind*.

14. Brooke's actions re-create two aspects of the liminality of Aphrodite as well as pinpoint the dilemma of the impermissible, sexual, active adult female (see Friedrich, 202-4, 219-20).

15. Anne Goodwyn Jones, "The World of Lee Smith," in *Women Writers of the Contemporary South*, ed. Peggy Whitman Prenshaw (Jackson: University of Mississippi Press, 1984), 257; hereafter cited in text as "Jones 1984."

16. Ring dancing is very old, and I am sure that I have not plumbed the possibilities of its meaning in this text. Note that Toni Morrison also evokes it in *Song of Solomon*.

17. See Susan Griffin, *Pornography and Silence: Culture's Revenge against Nature* (Berkeley: University of California Press, 1987); hereafter cited in text.

Chapter Four

1. *Fancy Strut* (New York: Harper & Row, 1973), 28; hereafter cited in text as *Strut*.

2. Carol Gilligan, "Oedipus and Psyche: Two Love Stories," paper read at MLA convention, Washington, D.C., December 1989; hereafter cited in text as "Gilligan 1989." Gilligan's theme is ultimately that which I am trying to get at in this book: "The key to the riddle of femininity – that is, to the mystification of women and women's silence – *is the hidden figure of woman as both lover and mother in stories about love*. It is the emergence of this figure as a perceiver and knower – a seer and a speaker rather than an object or mirror – that renders female development coherent and transforms the psychology of love. If women are known, then love becomes known as a relationship rather than a self-enclosed state" (Gilligan 1989, 24).

3. One of the best statements on the function and importance of the erotic is Audre Lorde's "Uses of the Erotic: The Erotic as Power," in *Sister Outsider: Essays and Speeches* (Trumansburg, N.Y.: Crossing Press, 1984). I am indebted to Dr. Kim Hall for calling my attention to this essay.

4. The angel who appears to Abou Ben Adhem in this poem holds a lily, perhaps signalling the presence of Aphrodite.

5. Marie-Louise von Franz, "The Process of Individuation," in *Man and His Symbols*, ed. Carl Jung (New York: Dell, 1964), 221; hereafter cited in text.

6. See Dorothee Soelle and Shirley A. Cloyes, *To Work and to Love: A Theology of Creation* (Philadelphia: Fortress, 1984), 138-39; and Mircea Eliade, *Images and Symbols* (New York: Sheed & Ward, 1969), 14.

Chapter Five

1. Lecture to contemporary literature class, University of North Carolina at Chapel Hill, March 1987; hereafter cited in text as "Lecture, 1987."

2. According to Marvin Perry et al. (in *Western Civilization*, vol 1. [to 1789], 2d ed. [Boston: Houghton Mifflin, 1985]), in addition to burying their dead, another belief of the Paleolithic peoples "is shown in the many small statues of women, made between 40,000 and 25,000 years ago, that have been found by archaeologists in Europe and Asia" (4; hereafter cited in text).

3. "The close association of females with nature may be panhuman, but that association need not exclude women from ultimate sanctity *unless* one locates ultimate sanctity outside of nature. Many polytheisms do not.

The Mediterranean monotheisms do; they elevate God beyond this world, and with that elevation women take a mythic fall" (Combs-Schilling, 256-57).

4. The repetition of the number three is not significant in the dominant Judeo-Christian iconography only. Proinsias MacCana points out that triplication is "a more or less universal feature of traditional thought" that "received particularly free and elaborate expression among the Celts" (*Celtic Mythology* [London: Hamlyn, 1970], 48-49). The literatures of Ireland and Wales show a "marked penchant for groups of three characters, and the significant thing about these groups is that very often they represent the triplication of a single personage." Triple goddesses were especially prevalent. Triads of goddesses included the

> formidable group who have a special claim on the title goddess of war. Though often appearing singly these are normally conceived as a trio. They generally comprise the Morríghan, "Phantom Queen," and *Badgh*, "Crow, Raven," accompanied by *Nembain*, "Frenzy" or by *Macha*. Since these goddesses are not infrequently identified with one another, the inference is that they are really the triplication of a single deity, and this is in fact corroborated by occasional references to the three Morríghans. Normally these war goddesses do not themselves engage in armed conflict: their weapons are the magic they command and the very terror which they inspire by their dread presence. (MacCana, 86)

Yet "the paps of the Morríghan" attest to the maternal function (MacCana, 94). See Adam McLean's *The Triple Goddess* for a further exploration of this theme. I am arguing that Red Emmy, Pricey Jane, and Dory comprise a triple goddess. The common representation of three witches only underscores the fate of the fallen goddess.

5. See Edward W. Said, *Orientalism* (New York: Vintage, 1979), 110-97; and Sander L. Gilman, "Black Bodies, White Bodies: Toward an Iconography of Female Sexuality in Late Nineteenth Century Art, Medicine, and Literature," *Critical Inquiry* 12 (Autumn 1985):204-42. For racial implications, note that Smith's Mrs. Darcy sees a blue-eyed savior in the vision that grants her the power of healing ("Mrs. Darcy Meets the Blue-Eyed Stranger at the Beach," *Carolina Quarterly* 30, no. 2 [Spring-Summer 1978]: 72).

6. See MacCana, *Celtic Mythology*: "*Epona*, 'The Divine Horse' or 'The Horse Goddess' was one of the more important Gaulish deities. . . . [S]ome scholars have seen an equivalent of her in the Welsh *Rbiannon*" (55). Further corroborative proof of Smith's interest in mining mythologies is provided in the list appearing in "Horses" under the title "Who Has Horses?":

1. The Four Horsemen of the Apocalypse.
2. Helios, whose horses pull the sun. These include Amethea (no loiterer) and Erythreos (red producer).

3. Pluto. One of his horses is named Abaster (away from the stars).
4. O'Donohue, whose horses are white waves that come on a windy day,
topped with foam. Every seventh year on May Day, O'Donohue himself reap-
pears and can be glimpsed gliding, to beautiful but wild music, over the lakes
of Killarney on his own white horse. Fairies with flowers precede him.
(*Cakewalk*, 208)

7. Joseph Campbell, *Primitive Mythology* (New York: Penguin, 1987),
428; hereafter cited in text as "Campbell 1987a."
8. Robert Graves, *Greek Myths*, vol. 1 (Baltimore: Penguin, 1957), 11;
hereafter cited in text.
9. This cultural phenomenon is not limited to Christian cultures.
Compare Sudhir Kakar, *Intimate Relations: Exploring Indian Sexuality*
(Chicago: University of Chicago Press, 1989): "Male terror of the female
sexual appetite shields itself by idealizing a woman's maternal role"(7).
10. Jean Markale, *Women of the Celts*, trans. A. Mygind, C. Hauch, and
P. Henry (Rochester, Vt.: Inner Traditions, 1986), 113; hereafter cited in
text. To make matters more complex, the Old Celtic *Morgan* (Muirgen)
probably means "born of the sea," recalling *Al marine*, as well as "the birth
of Aphrodite from the foam" (43). Despite her essentialist reading of "the
female," Markale's is a very useful work.
11. The original proto-Indo-European **dyews* (from whence "Zeus")
was a sky god strongly associated with stone (Friedrich, 216).
12. On Mary Magdalene, see Combs-Schilling, 91-92.
13. Joseph Campbell, *The Hero with a Thousand Faces* (Cleveland,
Ohio: Meridian, 1966), 105; hereafter cited in text as "Campbell 1966."
14. Anne Goodwyn Jones, "The Orality of *Oral History*," *Iron Mountain Review* 3, no. 1 (Winter 1986): 17; hereafter cited in text as "Jones
1986."
15. I am indebted for the identification of Vashti to Dr. Kenneth Craig.
16. George A. Buttrick, ed., *Interpreter's Dictionary of the Bible*, vol. 4
(Nashville, Tenn.: Abingdon Press, 1962), 746-47; hereafter cited in text.
17. The only other research, as far as I know, that identifies the mythic
stratum of Smith's work is that of Dr. Gloria Underwood. Her July 1991 dissertation at the University of South Carolina, "Blessings and Burdens:
Memory in the Novels of Lee Smith," identifies Little Luther: "Little Luther
Wade is Hephaestus: crippled, he works with his hands as a skilled crafts-
man. And his love for Dory parallels the love of Hephaestus for Venus"
(Ph.D. diss. draft, 70).
18. Carl Jung, "Answer to Job," In *The Portable Jung*, ed. Joseph
Campbell (New York: Viking, 1971), 643; Jung's italics.
19. I am grateful to the prurient mind of Patricia O'Connor for pointing out to me the meaning of Parrott's story, which I had missed.

20. According to Robert Graves, "One of the most uncompromising rejections of early Greek mythology was made by Socrates. Myths frightened or offended him; he preferred to turn his back on them and discipline his mind to think scientifically; 'to investigate the reason of the being of everything – of everything as it is, not as it appears, and to reject all opinions of which no account can be given'" (*The White Goddess* [New York: Farrar, Straus & Giroux, 1966], 10).

21. A humorous rendering of this dichotomization is given in *Black Mountain Breakdown*, in Crystal's scathing synopsis of a story by a former lover, a pretentious writer named Jerold Kukafka, which he explained as "an existential parable about a lost soul in modern America, killed in the end by that which seems to nourish . . . the bitch/mother image" (*Black*, 180-81).

22. Victor Turner, *The Ritual Process: Structure and Anti-Structure* (Ithaca, N.Y.: Cornell University Press, 1977).

23. Reading *Oral History* in my Liberal Studies class at Georgetown University in the fall of 1991, student John Poirier directed me to the story of Red Eva McMurrough. According to James Reynolds in *Ghosts in Irish Houses* (1947; rpt., New York: Bonanza Books, 1981),

> In all the bright roster of Gallic history, I'll wager there is no person accorded a background so magnificently caparisoned as Red Eva McMurrough, of Kilkenny Castle and Red Eva's Tower on the border of County Tipperary and County Limerick. The fortress of Kilkenny Castle belonged to The McMurrough, Eva's father. The border tower Red Eva built herself. She waged continuous war, and eventually lost her life defending the tower against the Quinns of Limerick.
>
> Schoolbooks make a great feature of Eva McMurrough being the "wife of Strongbow." She was that, of course. But the story of Red Eva blazes forth, up and down the land, in so many other forms that it takes your breath. She is said by historians to have been of titanic stature, and for some she has assumed a height towering out of all reason; one chronicler says Red Eva was eight feet tall. (81)

Red Eva is as pivotal historically (mythologically?) as Vashti. According to Lawrence John McCaffrey in *Ireland: From Colony to Nation State* (Englewood Cliffs, N.J.: Prentice-Hall, 1979),

> English imperialism in Ireland did not begin as a planned adventure, even though Ireland became England's first colony. English or Norman intervention in Ireland began when Dermot MacMurrough went to Wales in search of help to regain Leinster, which he had lost in the Irish civil war. He persuaded Richard fitz Gilbert de Clare, Earl of Pembroke, known as Strongbow, one of Henry II's vassals patrolling the Welsh frontier, to assist him. In exchange,

MacMurrough promised Strongbow his daughter in marriage and a succession
to the Leinster throne. (1)

In other words, the marriage of Red Eva McMurrough to "Strongbow"
marked the beginning of English domination. She goes down in legend as
the "mightiest woman in Ireland. . . . Her armor ran with blood, for the
hearts of men were stuck on prongs of iron. Iron spears that bristled across
her breast" (Reynolds, 87).

Red Eva's ghost taking the shape of a "red Kerry cow" (87) may suggest
that Red Emmy not only bewitched the cow but in fact was the cow, and
her jealousy the poison.

Note that in the mythological (i.e., oral) version the woman, Red Eva,
is the dominant character, while the historical version – although it gives
the full name, title, and nickname of her husband – only identifies her, in
relation to men, as McMurrough's daughter.

Chapter Six

1. Dorothy Dinnerstein, *The Mermaid and the Minotaur: Sexual Arrangements and Human Malaise* (New York: Harper & Row, 1976), 275.

2. The title of the novel *The Go-between* (1953) should alert us to the
presence of Aphrodite. In that novel, a boy sees a beautiful woman in the
sex act, in full orgasmic cry, and it sets a stamp on his life.

3. According to Patricia Monaghan in *Book of Goddesses and Heroines*, rev. ed. (St. Paul, Minn.: Llewellyn, 1991),

Mor meant "sea" in several Celtic languages, and Morgan was a sea-goddess
whose name still survives in Brittany, where sea sprites are called morgans.
The most famous sea-goddess was surnamed Le Fay; in Welsh mythology she
was said to be a queen of Avalon, the underworld fairyland where King Arthur
was carried – some said by Morgan – when he disappeared from this world. In
some legends, Morgan was Arthur's sister, whereas in other tales she was immortal, living with her eight sisters in Avalon, where she was an artist and a
healer.

Some scholars claim she was the same goddess as the one called, in Ireland, Great Queen Morrigan. That crow-headed goddess was a battle divinity,
which suggests that Morgan might also have been a goddess of death. Indeed,
there is dispute over whether her surname means "the fairy" or "the fate." If
Morgan was not a mere sea sprite but the goddess of death, that would explain her unfriendly character in Malory's *Morte d'Arthur*, where Morgan appears as the king's dreaded foe. If Morgan was once the queen of death, ruler
of the underworld and of rebirth to the early Britons, a cultural shift could
easily have seen her reinterpreted as a powerful demonic force bent on destruction. (241-42)

4. "Neti was instructed to open to the queen of heaven th seven gates, but to abide by the custom and remove at each portal a part of her clothing. . . . The naked goddess hung on a stake for three days before being rescued" (Campbell 1987a, 106). "Neti" (Nettie?), then, was the gatekeeper of Inanna's sister and enemy, Ereshkigal. Inanna, prefiguring Christ, descends into hell for three days, where, stripped of her clothes, she hangs on a stake: "The oldest recorded account of the passage through the gates of metamorphosis is the Sumerian myth of the goddess Inanna's descent to the netherworld" (Campbell 1987a, 105).

5. "Aphrodite and Hermes were linked ritually at a number of cult centers and seem closer to each other in overall gestalt than either is to any other deity" (Friedrich, 92). "The details of Hermes' liminality have been clarified by Otto. . . . Small wonder that he and Aphrodite were eventually synthesized as the Hermaphrodite figure of classical and Hellenistic times" (Friedrich, 205). Note, however, that the original Celtic/Old Irish Mercury–like the precursors of Inanna–had much wider interests, including war (MacCana, 27), and, perhaps importantly for our author, he was a *smith* (MacCana, 28).

6. *Family Linen* (New York: G. P. Putnam's Sons, 1985), 35; hereafter cited in text as *Linen.*

7. "Intensive Care" also has a beautiful redheaded heroine–this one named Cherry Oxendine–whose husband, Harold, never forgets the same primal scene that marks Almarine for life in *Oral History.* At their high school senior class picnic, Harold pulls an inebriated Cherry out of the lake. Like Red Emmy, she makes no move to cover her glory: "She took his shirt and put it on, tying it stylishly at the waist" (*Eclipse,* 175). All the time "Ramblin' Rose" is playing on the radio, in case we hadn't noticed that our goddess of many names was near. Harold, like Almarine, has seen the goddess naked. In the story, still a beautiful woman, she is "drowning" as her lungs fill with water.

8. Islands are interstitial, thus places for temples of Aphrodite; and note Cherry Oxendine of "Intensive Care" "drowning."

9. See Sander Gilman on the conflation of black, southern and female in *Difference and Pathology: Stereotypes of Sexuality, Race, and Madness* (Ithaca, N.Y.: Cornell University Press, 1985), and "Black Bodies, White Bodies."

10. Michelle Lodge, "PW Interviews: Lee Smith," *Publishers Weekly,* 20 September 1985, 110.

Chapter Seven

1. Vicki Covington, "Hail to Lee Smith and Ivy Rowe and the Courage to Write," *Atlanta Journal and Constitution,* 25 September 1988, 11; hereafter cited in text.

2. Roz Kaveney, "In the South," *Times Literary Supplement*, 21-27 July 1989, 803; hereafter cited in text.

3. Joseph Campbell, *Creative Mythology* (New York: Penguin, 1976), 109; hereafter cited in text as "Campbell 1987b."

4. According to Diane Ackerman, "We like to think that we are finely evolved creatures, in suit-and-tie or pantyhose-and-chemise, who live many millennia and mental detours away from the cave, but that's not something our bodies are convinced of" (*A Natural History of the Senses* [New York: Random House, 1990], xxvii).

5. According to Monaghan, "All these apparent contradictions cease to be problematical, however, if one extends the 'three persons in one god' concept to this trinity of Sumerian divinities. They've seen that the mother, the lover, and the sister were all aspects of a single grand figure: the queen of heaven" (Monaghan, 150).

6. Going back to the split between sex and language I discuss in Chapter 3 (when Crystal is raped), note:

> At a deeper level there is an association between gold, honey, speech, and sexual fluids, as we find in Slavic (especially gold/honey) and Indic (gold/semen). As for gold/speech, the entire phrase "speech sweeter than honey" is . . . one of the relatively complex syntactic units that we can reconstruct with complete confidence for Proto-Indo-European because of point-for-point correspondences between the strings of words in Greek, Celtic, (Old Irish), Anatolian, and yet other languages. . . . Gold and its semantic cognates in speech, honey, and semen therefore symbolize the yet deeper Aphrodite values of procreation, verbal creation, and so forth. There are more strands to this skein, but I think what I have out so far should suggest the richness and complexity of the supposedly "simple" epithet "golden." (Friedrich, 79)

7. Kathryn Stripling Byer, "Weep-Willow," collected in *Wildwood Flower* (Baton Rouge: Louisiana State University Press, forthcoming).

Chapter Eight

1. See Carolyn G. Heilbrun, *Writing a Woman's Life* (New York: Norton, 1988).

2. See William Barrett, *Death of the Soul: From Descartes to the Computer* (Garden City, N.Y.: Anchor, 1987); Griffin, *Pornography and Silence*; Carol Gilligan, *In a Different Voice: Psychological Theory and Women's Development* (Cambridge, Mass: Harvard University Press, 1982).

3. See Sherry B. Ortner, "Is Female to Male as Nature Is to Culture?," in *Woman, Culture, and Society*, ed. Michelle Rosaldo and Louise Lamphere (Stanford, Calif.: Stanford University Press, 1974); and Griffin, *Pornography and Silence*.

4. Diane Wolkstein and Samuel Noah Kramer, *Inanna, Queen of Heaven and Earth: Her Stories and Hymns from Sumer* (New York: Harper & Row, 1983), 53.

5. Judith Thurman, "When You Wish upon a Star," *New Yorker*, 29 May 1989, 108.

6. Alfred North Whitehead, *Science and the Modern World* (New York: Mentor Books, 1948).

7. Jayne Anne Phillips, *Fast Lanes* (New York: Dutton/Seymour Lawrence, 1987), 101.

Selected Bibliography

PRIMARY SOURCES

Novels

Black Mountain Breakdown. New York: G. P. Putnam's Sons, 1980.
Fair and Tender Ladies. New York: G. P. Putnam's Sons, 1988.
Family Linen. New York: G. P. Putnam's Sons, 1985.
Fancy Strut. New York: Harper & Row, 1973.
The Last Day the Dogbushes Bloomed. New York: Harper & Row, 1968.
Oral History. New York: G. P. Putnam's Sons, 1983.
Something in the Wind. New York: Harper & Row, 1971.

Collected Short Stories

Cakewalk. New York: G. P. Putnam's Sons, 1981. Nine of the stories first appeared in the following magazines: "Artists" and "All the Days of Our Lives" in *Redbook*; "Georgia Rose" in *McCall's*; "The French Revolution: A Love Story" in *Ingenue*; and "Heat Lightning," "Between the Lines," and "Mrs. Darcy Meets the Blue-eyed Stranger at the Beach" in *Carolina Quarterly*. "Horses" originally appeared in *Love Stories by New Women* (Charlotte, N.C.: Red Clay Books, 1978).
Me and My Baby View the Eclipse. New York: G. P. Putnam's Sons, 1990. Four of the stories appeared, some in slightly different form, in the following magazines: "Life on the Moon" (as "Good-bye, Sweetheart") and "Me and My Baby View the Eclipse" in *Redbook*; "The Interpretation of Dreams" in *Southern Magazine*; and "Intensive Care" in *Special Report*. "Bob, a Dog" was published in a limited edition by Mud Puppy Press, Chapel Hill, North Carolina, in 1988.

Nonfiction

"Loose Characters" (review of Ellen Gilchrist's *Drunk with Love*). *Spectator*, 6-12 November 1986, 5.
"The Voice behind the Story." In *Voicelust: Eight Contemporary Fiction Writers on Style*, edited by Allen Wier and Don Hendrie, Jr. Lincoln: University of Nebraska Press, 1985.

SECONDARY SOURCES

Biography

Kearns, Katherine. "Lee Smith." In *Dictionary of Literary Biography Yearbook: 1983*, pp. 314-24. Detroit: Gale Research Co., 1984. An excellent summary of Smith's work that breaks out of the usual parameters of this forum.

Interviews

Arnold, Edwin T. "An Interview with Lee Smith." *Appalachian Journal* 11 (Spring 1984): 240-54.

Hill, Dorothy Combs. "Interview with Lee Smith." *Southern Quarterly* 28, no. 2 (Winter 1990): 5-19.

Lodge, Michelle. "PW Interviews: Lee Smith." *Publishers Weekly*, 20 September 1985, 110-11.

Lyons, Gene. "The South Rises Again." *Newsweek*, 30 September 1985, 71-74B.

Scandling, Mark. "Staying in Touch with the Real World." *Carolina Quarterly* 32, no. 1 (Winter 1980): 51-57.

Smith, Virginia A. "On Regionalism, Women's Writing, and Writing as a Woman: A Conversation with Lee Smith." *Southern Review* 26 (1990): 784-95.

"A Stubborn Sense of Place." *Harper's*, August 1986, 35.

Criticism

Broadwell, Elizabeth. "Lee Smith." In *New Writers of the South*, edited by Joseph M. Flora and Robert Bain. Westport, Conn.: Greenwood Press, 1991. Thoughtful exposition. Biography, major themes, and survey of criticism.

Dale, Corinne. "The Power of Language in Lee Smith's *Oral History*." *Southern Quarterly* 28, no. 2 (Winter 1990): 21-34. A successful application of the theories of Lacan and Kristeva to Smith's fiction. This linguistic study concludes that Smith succeeds in constructing a subversive narrative that can properly be called "the mother tongue."

Jennings, Ben. "Language and Reality in Lee Smith's *Oral History*." *Iron Mountain Review* 3, no. 1 (Winter 1986): 10-14. An invaluable sociolinguistic study of language in *Oral History*.

Jones, Anne Goodwyn. "The Orality of *Oral History*." *Iron Mountain Review* 3, no. 1 (Winter 1986): 15-19. Groundbreaking study of the sacred-sexual connotations of *Oral History*.

_____. "The World of Lee Smith." In *Women Writers of the Contemporary South*, edited by Peggy Whitman Prenshaw, pp. 249-72. Jackson:

University of Mississippi Press, 1984. Brilliant analysis of the technical virtuosity and themes in the corpus of Smith's work through *Oral History*.

Kearns, Katherine. "From Shadow to Substance: The Empowerment of the Artist Figure in Lee Smith's Fiction." In *Writing the Woman Artist*, edited by Suzanne W. Jones, pp. 175-95. Philadelphia: University of Pennsylvania Press, 1991. A perceptive and lyrical unraveling of the conflict between mother and artist roles in Smith's fiction.

MacKethan, Lucinda H. "Artists and Beauticians: Balance in Lee Smith's Fiction." *Southern Literary Journal* 15 (Fall 1982): 3-14. One of the first studies to grasp Smith's ethos.

Rogoff, Leonard. *Carolina Quarterly* 26, no. 1 (1974): 110-14. One of the most perceptive early reviews of Smith's work.

Soos, Frank. "Insiders and Outsiders: Point of View in Lee Smith's *Oral History*." *Iron Mountain Review* 3, no. 1 (Winter 1986): 20-24. Exploration of Smith's use of point of view highlighting what it means to go into and out of the mountains or to belong there.

Index

The Author

Dorothy Combs Hill received her Ph.D. in English from the University of North Carolina at Chapel Hill in 1988 and her M.A. from Middlebury College's Bread Loaf School of English in 1977. During her editorship of the *Carolina Quarterly*, the magazine won two O. Henry Awards and a Best American Short Story Award. Her interviews with Lee Smith and Bobbie Ann Mason appear in the *Southern Quarterly*, her interview with Jayne Anne Phillips in the *South Carolina Review*. Currently teaching at Georgetown University, Professor Hill is working on a book entitled *The Female Imagination*.

ACJ-4300

3/31/92
S.D.

PS
3569
M5376
Z68
1992